"What Actually Happens"

"WHAT ACTUALLY HAPPENS"

The Representation of Real-World Phenomena

by

Peter G. Ossorio

UNIVERSITY OF SOUTH CAROLINA PRESS
Columbia, South Carolina

Library of Congress Cataloging in Publication Data

Ossorio, Peter G
  "What actually happens."
  Bibliography: p.
  Includes index.
  1. Psychology—Methodology. I. Title.
[DNLM: 1. Behavior. 2. Psychology. 3. Metaphysics
4. Perception. BF311   084w]
BF38.5.083 1978   128'.2   78–14967
ISBN 0–87249–365–2

CONTENTS

•

TABLES

PREFACE

•

Sometimes it is better just to make a fresh start.

Just as a building may be so ramshackle that it can neither bear the weight it must nor be refurbished or enlarged effectively, so also may a social or intellectual structure be so deficient and self-defeating that any procedure which involved accepting it in general in order to correct some deficiencies in particular would be as hopeful and productive as slapping Uncle Remus's Tar Baby around. In such circumstances one naturally tries to salvage what one can, but a fresh start is indicated.

I take this to be evidently the case with the social and intellectual institutions which have come to be self-characterized as "behavioral science" and, further, with the more general social-intellectual structure within which "behavioral science" is carried on. Under the former heading I include at least (1) a miscellaneous collection of behavioral theories and models, including the psychoanalytic, phenomenological, cognitive-developmental, S-R, physiological, "systems," and "miniature theory" genres, and (2) a miscellaneous body of customs and practices, one among which is to give some of the others such honorific designations as "methodology," "meta-theory," "experimental design," and so on. Under the latter heading I would include at least the disciplines of philosophy of science, semantic theory, moral philosophy, metaphysics, ontology, epistemology, and philosophy of mind.

I report these as observations, not as a bill of particulars, for I do not intend to come to cuffs with that Tar Baby. Part of what is involved in making a fresh start is that I shall not survey or critically examine the most nearly related work in behavioral science or philosophy as it now exists, except occasionally, and then for heuristic purposes, not scholarly ones. The work of introducing an alternative intellectual climate and conceptual idiom must precede any work of comparison and appraisal. Moreover, it may be advisable to leave these later tasks to others.

The Tar Baby problem may be put in this form: Any present critical survey or critical analysis of theories or theses within the traditional intellectual structure could be accomplished only by recourse to theories, disciplines, vocabularies, customs, or norms within the same general structure and would therefore be vitiated by the deficiencies of the structure as a whole and at these points. And any attempt to clear up *these* difficulties would face the same problem. And so on. The more we struggle with the deformities and deficiencies of our traditional intellectual framework, the more we are stuck with it. Since there appears to be no way out, the prudential course is not to get in. If there is an alternative, we do not have to get in.

It is a general feature of traditions and ways of thinking that in-house technical criticism will be provided for, and even encouraged, whereas fundamental criticism will appear to be wrongheaded, incomprehensible, naive, or blindly antagonistic, except within an alternative outlook. It is not merely that to a tic-tac-toe player the world consists of noughts and crosses. It is also that his ultimate standard of criticism and the ultimate form of his reality testing is "But will it get me three in a row?" The way to avoid this particular form of self-validation is to do something else instead.

x

By a "fresh start" I do not mean anything very dramatic or exotic. The reference is essentially to a procedure and only consequently to a product. The procedure is simply to be directly responsive to the fact of persons and behavior and to our intellectual, practical, and scientific needs in respect to them and to give these concerns complete priority over any concern for preserving traditional or current scientific or philosophical theories, methodologies, vocabularies, customs, practices, or social norms. I do not, therefore, in any way wish to suggest that the alternative outlook I shall present has no connection and no resemblance to anything at all in our intellectual and scientific history or that it could not be categorized within any of the traditional taxonomies. At most, I should want to suggest that to understand it primarily in such terms is to miss the point *entirely*.

I shall be concerned primarily with the presentation of an alternative outlook. I take it that most of those who can see or sense that there is something fundamentally defective in the way we have gone about our efforts at a behavioral science are properly more concerned with an alternative that is not hopeless than they are with an impeccable demonstration of what it is that has gone wrong. And since understanding the alternative involves not only mastering some explicit formulations but also acquiring some level of implicit competence ("tacit knowledge," "apperceptive mass," "know-how," etc.), I have chosen for this presentation the relatively free form of a monograph, or extended essay, rather than a more mannered academic form such as would be appropriate for an introductory textbook, a theoretical presentation, a philosophical argument, a critical review, or a technical exposition.

Formally, the alternative is a single complex concept, or conceptual system, in which we can distinguish four major, logically interrelated components. The overall concept is currently designated as the "Human Model" or "Person Concept." (At various times I have referred to it as the "Behavioral Model," "Intentional Action System," "Reality System," and "Three-system System." There does not seem to be a really satisfactory term to use here.) The four major components are the concepts of Reality, Person, Behavior, and Language. The social enterprise of generating and using these and related formulations as technical resources in a behavioral science has been consistently designated as "Descriptive Psychology." I expect that at least three monographs will be necessary for a minimum presentation of the Person Concept. Of these, the present volume deals with reality concepts. As now envisaged the second will deal with persons and behavior. The third will deal with language and science. The fourth and subsequent volumes will deal with behavior theories, status dynamics, personality assessment, psychopathology, personal change, and other topics.

Because of its complexity and scope, I do not believe it is possible to give a satisfactory orienting characterization of the Human Model any more than it is possible to give a perspicuous characterization of the general intellectual and human outlook to which it provides an alternative. Instead, I will simply warn against approaching it or reflecting upon it as though it were a familiar something such as a psychological theory, a metatheory, an experimental methodology, a metaphysics, a philosophy of science, a system of psychotherapy, a piece of linguistic analysis or conceptual analysis, an axiomatic formal system, et cetera. It is not a way of getting three in a row.

Obviously, any claim to be offering an alternative of the scope suggested above will smack of grandiosity. I make no apologies for that. It is highly unlikely that any such alternative would be recognized as being of this kind if it were not presented as *sui generis* and with suitable disclaimers, for nothing could be more inevitable than for a member of la dolce vita academica to recognize it as a familiar nought or cross and treat it accordingly.

Perhaps the most that can be done here is to call attention to the kind of difficulties, ambiguities, and temptations to which the reader will be exposed in the course of the presentation. Most of these are captured elegantly in the classic two-liner:

Gil: Do you believe in baptism?
Wil: Believe in it? Man, I've seen it done!

I am presenting an alternative, not describing one or arguing that there is one.

One of the novel features of the presentation of the Person Concept is that, although it involves many declarative sentences, it does not involve making statements or assertions. Instead, what I shall be doing with those verbal performances is (a) delineating concepts, i.e., *constructing* or *exhibiting* forms of representation (corresponding to articulated concepts), or else (b) *illustrating* the use of these concepts in behavioral science both as pre-empirical foundations and workaday technical resources for empirical and explanatory efforts. (Note that doing the first of these is a way of doing the latter and that frequently the reverse is the case.) Thus, unlike the usual technical exposition, the presentation is one for which questions of truth cannot arise (logically cannot arise, since concepts cannot be true or false and neither can behaviors). Rather, questions about the truth of any statement presuppose the Person Concept or some equivalent thereof, since it is only within such a framework that any such question can be formulated, understood, reacted to, or acted upon.

The form of presentation is something of a necessity. Concepts cannot be told, nor can they be stated. This is a concomitant of their not having any possible truth value. Further, unlike the case of presenting a thesis or a theory to an audience, the presentation of a concept is a rare undertaking, and there is no conventional or reliable way to accomplish it. In general, if one does anything, one teaches concepts rather than presents them. The task of presenting a concept is, in Cavell's phrase, the task of getting someone to see, and that falls in some unknown region between teaching and telling. Generally, technical concepts are presented in the form of (and incidental to) a set of paradigmatically True statements which make up a theory or model. The use of these concepts is, therefore, preempted by the paradigmatic statements, and that is reasonable because for such concepts those verbal paradigms do indeed define their use as technical terms. In the present case it is of critical importance not to preempt either the use of the central concepts or the truth about the real world in this way. The central concepts are not invented technical concepts, and their primary use is neither in verbal behavior nor in the search for truth. Hence the reliance on illustration rather than definition and on the general behavioral use of language rather than its specifically statement-making use. (The systematic formulation of language as a form of behavior will be given in a subsequent monograph.)

Just as concepts cannot have truth values, neither can they have assumptions or presuppositions, and the present behavioral form of presentation is in accordance with this limitation. The procedure illustrates an alternative to the traditional academic folk wisdom which has it that "You have to make *some* assumptions." Heuristically, the procedure provides a kind of antidote to the myopic preoccupation with Truth and deduction which is endemic to philosophers and experimental technicians. Such a preoccupation would be a severe handicap in understanding the Human Model. After all, there is nothing there that could be believed—or doubted.

The preoccupation with Truth is not merely a handicap. It leads to many incidents of the Wil and Gil variety. For example, typically, a philosopher who encounters some portion of the Person Concept will do more or less the following. (1) He will invent some statements which are being made, and he will be (properly) dubious of their Truth value. (2) He will invent some assumptions or presuppositions which 'underlie' these statements, and he will be (properly) dubious about their Truth value also. (3) He will categorize the 'theory' under one of the traditional philosophical rubrics (which one depends on who is doing the categorizing; they have ranged from idealism to behaviorism). (4) He will condemn or disdain the 'theory' on the grounds that that *kind* of theory encounters known difficulties. Since all existing philosophical theories are criticizable in this way that is not a risky judgment. (5) He will disdain the whole enterprise as philosophically naive (because it was not presented under the philosophical rubric, because it's naive to think that philosophy offers fundamental answers or solutions, and because everybody knows there's nothing new under the sun). Or else he will condemn the enterprise as evasive or disingenuous, because you *have* to be making assumptions, and anyone who denies it has got to be joking, or, . . . , et cetera. (6) Finally, he will ignore warnings to the effect that he is completely off target (for he knows better than that) or he will address himself to such warnings as naive or disingenuous *statements*. Having got three in a row, he retires from the field.

There are exceptions, of course, but they are not frequent among American philosophers. We may note the incidence of such imperviousness, but without a common ground, e.g., in competence, coercion, or good faith, there appears to be no effective way to get around it. Indeed, such a transcendent and savage attachment to Truth is perhaps best left untouched by merely human agency. What we can do is to go on about our business as behavioral scientists and keep somewhere in mind the moral that our past preoccupations with Truth (no less in denying it than in searching for it) have limited our understanding of the real world and thereby limited severely the kinds of truth we have thought to inquire about empirically and the ways in which we have gone about the inquiry.

Ordinarily, to present a single monograph as the first of four or five is to invite the judgment that one is trying to live off promissory notes as though they were hard cash. I do not have any qualms of this kind about such a commitment. Descriptive Psychology is an actuality, not an IOU. Most of the material for these volumes is already at hand, and most of that has borne from three to ten years of criticism and revision in consultation with students and colleagues. Several partial or preliminary formulations have been published previously and others have been in existence for years as instructional materials. For example, the transition rule formulation of the reality concepts (Section II of the present volume) was initially accomplished in 1964 in connection with the original draft of "Persons," being published for limited circulation in 1966, and the three-element formula for verbal behavior had already been achieved in 1962.

It is characteristic of Descriptive Psychology that, although systematization is insisted upon, a priori formalization is resisted. Typically, the descriptive and notational system has been extended by first dealing successfully with a conceptual, clinical, or experimental problem, then asking in retrospect "What did we do that was decisive?" and only later systematizing and extending the answer and using it elsewhere. For example, the reality formats introduced in Section III of the present volume reflect a solution to some technical problems in optimizing communications networks and in providing computer systems with functional self-knowledge; similarly, the "theory of empiricism" presented in Section III and elsewhere is partly a development in the field of "status dynamics," which in turn is an outgrowth of a conceptual analysis and therapeutic strategy for dealing with clinical depression; likewise, the calculational formulation of the concept of behavior to be presented in Volume II stems from the ad hoc use of a defective form of behavior description in analyzing and comparing apparently incommensurable theories of schizogenic family interaction. Thus "the system" has grown in a fragmentary and saltatory way, with reconciliation and dovetailing of the disparate elements coming generally after the fact and with some unexpected rewards. Descriptive Psychology is primarily an intellectual and human outlook, competence, and enterprise, not a verbal technology; and it is from that outlook and competence that the various phenomena of behavior and persons can be dealt with, codified, and understood.

The field is developing at a sufficiently rapid pace to make a definitive summary of the state of the art impossible. As a result of recent developments an up-to-date systematization of the Person Concept is due. And one might say that a comprehensive presentation of some fundamentals to a general audience is long overdue. This tardiness is not accidental. If its practitioners are unanimous about anything it is that although Descriptive Psychology is effective and rewarding as a way of being an intellectually responsible scientific practitioner (clinician, experimenter, teacher), it is painful and unrewarding as a subject matter for a merely discursive presentation to any kind of traditional audience. Indeed, if one had to assume that such an effort would be substantially successful in order for it to make sense to try, no such effort would be forthcoming. Thus, it is after some years of delay and with some distaste and serious reservations that I have undertaken the systematic presentation. Since public commitment increases the likelihood of performance, it seems advisable to make the commitment public and to begin now.

P. G. O.
1976

"What Actually Happens"

Abbreviations

Basic Object Unit	BOU
Basic Process Unit	BPU
Limiting Case	LC
Object Name	O-Name
Object Paradigm	O-Paradigm
Process Name	P-Name
State of Affairs	SA
State-of-Affairs Name	SA-Name
State-of-Affairs Unit	SAU

I

"WHAT ACTUALLY HAPPENS"

•

ONTOLOGY IS THE DISCIPLINE that studies Being, and one would suppose that the empirically oriented scientist must in principle have some interest and something fundamentally at stake in such matters. He does. But the philosopher's interest in Being is not the same as the scientist's interest in what is the case. "Being" is philosophers' jargon, and ontology is a philosopher's game, and neither has been found to be particularly apropos from a scientific point of view. I agree. Accordingly, in delineating what is of interest and what is at stake scientifically, I shall talk not about Being or Existence but about reality, reality concepts, and the real world. It does not come to the same thing.

At the present time it has become essential for behavioral scientists to deal with reality and reality concepts explicitly and systematically rather than by simple intuition or by "letting George do it." Traditionally, George has been the ontologist, the epistemologist, the philosopher of science, the physicist, and a variety of others, and the current state of the art in behavioral science directly reflects that intellectual default. Fortunately, there appears to be no difficulty in principle in regard to this necessary task. It does appear, however, that a full appreciation of the necessity is likely to follow, rather than to precede, a detailed understanding of how the requirement can, in fact, be met. The primary purpose of this presen-

3

tation is to contribute to such understanding by dealing explicitly and systematically with reality and reality concepts in a scientifically viable way.

It is essential to deal with reality explicitly because it has an essential relation to science, and it is essential to deal with it systematically because the relation is neither single nor simple.

As soon as we begin to consider what connections there are between the real world and the social institution of empirical science, at least three fundamental sorts of connection—methodological, substantive, and historical—come readily to mind. These connections make a difference at all levels from basic methodology to theorizing to experimental procedures to analysis and interpretation of data. Because of this, it is difficult to imagine how we could have an intellectually responsible behavioral science or a methodologically sound one or a substantively adequate one if we could not deal effectively with these connections within the scope of that science. To be sure, this is an unprecedented requirement to place on a science; but, then, it is hardly a feat of daring today to suggest that *obviously* a behavioral science would have to take a form which was unprecedented in some major respects if it were to be a science and not merely an agglomeration of behavior-manipulating and explanation-constructing techniques and practices.

The methodological, substantive, and historical connections between science and the real world may be summarized respectively, by saying that (a) science is empirical, (b) the real world is what scientific accounts are about, and (c) the scientific enterprise is a part of the history of the real world. These summaries may be elaborated briefly as follows:

A. THE METHODOLOGICAL CONNECTION

This connection between science and the real world involves the status that scientific statements have in our common life, and this in turn reflects the place that scientific procedures have in our common life.

The reference to the status of statements is perhaps unfamiliar. We are wont to think that statements simply *are* true or false, correct or incorrect, accurate or inaccurate, and so forth. We would normally say that a statement is true if what it states is the case; otherwise, it is not true. Truth depends on reality. (Note here the basis for a later technical strategy in which the notion of making truth appraisals and acting on beliefs is bypassed in favor of the notion of acting on reality concepts.)

There is a difference between what is real and what is merely a possibility. There is also a difference between what is factual and what is merely conjectural. Likewise, there is a difference between facts that could not be otherwise and facts which must be discovered to be the case. And so on. There is a whole family of cases here.

Correspondingly, there are differences among the linguistic expressions we give to these facts in our talk about such matters. There is a difference between a statement that is true and one that is not necessarily false. Likewise, there is a difference between a conclusion which is supported by the facts and one which is mere guesswork. And there is a difference between a statement which could not be false and one which merely happens to be true.

But which statements are which? The answer to this question cannot be read off from the statements themselves. The differences in question are differences in the methodological status of the statements in question, and no statement can simply confer a particular status on itself. Rather, we *give* the status of "true," "confirmed," "empirical," etc., to a statement by virtue of accepting it as, or taking it to be, "true," "confirmed," "empirical," etc.

To be sure, there are some linguistic conventions for making status assignments overtly. For example, "It is certain that such and such" and "It has been experimentally demonstrated that such

5

and such" are conventional ways of assigning particular statuses to the statement that such and such. But on a given occasion "It is certain that such and such" may be the expression of doubt, and in all cases it is up to the listener to accept or reject such and such as being certain. Likewise, it is up to the listener or reader to accept or not accept such and such as having been experimentally demonstrated.

It is because status assignments are in this way independent of the content of the statements which are appraised that we have been able to think of the methodological principles of science as something quite apart from the substantive content of scientific theories. Correspondingly, we have a picture of a "theoretically neutral" scientific method which is "applied to" various subject matters, including behavior, and which provides the criterion for whether the results of that application are (have the status of) *science*.

In general, to assign a status to a statement or a body of statements is to give it a place within a wider context in which it has some relevance. The point of making a status assignment is that it is an appraisal which carries putative implications in regard to behavioral possibilities, practicalities, or necessities—implications, that is, as to how it would make sense to act on that statement. For example, to treat a conjecture as though it were a fact would be injudicious as a policy and often impossible in point of fact. Equally, it would be rash to take a statistically significant finding as ipso facto an important one or to take an experimental conclusion either as simple truth or as being no different from the result of casual observation.

To say that science is empirical is to make a status assignment, albeit elliptically, of a general sort.

To say that science is empirical is to call attention to the fact that a major point of that social enterprise is to deal systematically and effectively with the kind of fact which must be discovered to be the case. (I shall later want to suggest that "predict and control" is a technician's parochial rendering of "deal effectively with.") Correspondingly, it is to remind us that scientific findings are established by observation and that scientific explanations (given that they qualify as explanations at all) are criticized to a large extent by reference to such findings, and that this is so *just because* the scientific enterprise deals essentially with this world, i.e., the real world, rather than with all possible worlds or with *merely possible* worlds. Scientific accounts have that kind of standing and that kind of putative value.

That science is empirical in this sense has, if anything, been overemphasized in the traditional and influential accounts of scientific practice. Yet, in spite of this emphasis, these accounts fall short of an adequate explication of the methodological connection between science and the real world, and they fall short in at least two major ways.

1. Scientific practice does indeed include empirical procedures as indispensable. But its doing so is a nonempirical methodological principle. We do not engage in empirical procedures in order to decide whether empirical procedures are essential to the scientific enterprise. No more do we conduct experiments to establish empirically what the essential characteristics of an experiment are. Empiricism is a procedural principle which can be followed sensibly only if it is adopted as (is given the status of) a nonempirical principle (see Section III, below). But no satisfactory presentation of a nonarbitrary pre-empirical basis for empirical procedures is included in traditional accounts of the matter.

2. Scientific findings are established by observation, and so that relationship is clear. But the relation of scientific theories to observation and to the real world has not been made clear despite

determined philosophical efforts. In the main, philosophies of science have been essentially reconstructions of the history of physics and related sciences (for perhaps the single exception, see Harré and Secord, 1973). But as we shall see shortly, the methodological requirements for a behavioral science are fundamentally different from those for a physical science. For a behavioral science, therefore, traditional philosophical theories concerning science are simply irrelevant. But if they provide us with no help, at least we need not be detained by them.

In summary, the methodological connection between science and the real world involves the empirical character of science. "How is science empirical?" is an old question, but our traditional approaches have not produced answers which are satisfactory in principle and deal with the issue in a fundamental way. We have not dealt effectively with the methodological connection either in our scientific theories of behavior or in our "methodological" theories of scientific behavior.

B. THE SUBSTANTIVE CONNECTION

This connection involves the factual content of scientific accounts. The real world is what scientific accounts are accounts *of*. This holds for both observational accounts and explanatory ones and for true accounts and fallacious ones. On this basis, one might expect that the concept of the real world would be an integral part of the substantive content of observational and explanatory scientific accounts. I need hardly say that on the face of it nothing of the sort occurs.

One explanation for this disparity is that the term "real world" is generally taken to refer to a purely methodological status (of the kind noted above). From this view it follows that "real world" is lacking in any substantive content. Such a conclusion might be argued for on the grounds that any such content could only consist of nonscientific, a priori speculation, since to the extent that the "real world" has any substantive content that is what is provided by the products of scientific effort, forever tentative though they may be. Closely associated with these views is the notion that reference to the conjectural entities ("hypothetical constructs") of explanatory scientific accounts is in principle a legitimate replacement for our "prescientific" references to the real world.

Such historical conceits are most easily held if one ignores the historical aspects of science. Conceit or not, it leaves both our observational terminology and our theoretical terminology without any intelligible connection to reality since the former is stipulated to be inadequate (else why would we need any scientific theories at all?) and the latter is in principle uncertain (not only because any particular account is open to revision, but because scientific accounts cannot certify their own status). Little wonder, then, that the ascendancy of such traditional views has resulted in a behavioral science which is fragmented, disoriented, and lacking in either foundations or fundamental behavioral concepts.

I have pointed out at some length elsewhere (1968, 1971) that the only existing theories of behavior which deal with scientific behavior *as such* are nonscientific, anecdotal theories of limited scope called "philosophy of science," the substantive content of which is incompatible with the content of scientific theories which purport to "apply to" *all* behavior. Yet these philosophical theories are indispensable to traditional empirical science since they provide the fundamentals of empirical procedures and of the traditional forms of scientific theorizing. After all, neither empirical procedures nor the accepted forms of scientific theorizing are capable of providing their own foundations or rationale. Neither, to date, has the philosophy of science been able to do this, and there is no reason to think it can. (Nor, of course, does philosophy of science provide

9

its own foundations.) Both theory and practice in current science are therefore necessarily incomplete in a methodological sense and in a fundamental way.

In considering the "content-free" argument, one might argue that although the concept of "the real world" is indeed lacking in any empirical factual content, since we have to find out about it by observation, it must nevertheless have a considerable amount of conceptual content, since without that we would have no basis for saying that any discovery or observation had anything at all to do with the real world. Since statements of fact, whether they be empirical or nonempirical, observational or explanatory, all require conceptual distinctions, one might then all the more expect that the *concept* of the real world would be an integral *conceptual* part of the substantive content of observational and explanatory scientific accounts of the real world and that a suitably articulated delineation of the concept of the real world would show where and how this was the case. Conceptual content of this sort would also be a *prima facie* candidate for providing the pre-empirical basis for the empirical procedures of a scientific enterprise. We will return to these notions in later sections.

C. THE HISTORICAL CONNECTION

The practice of science, including observing, explaining, and summarizing and organizing data and theory, occurs *within* the real world and is part of the real world. This is the force of saying that empirical science is a social institution (an organized body of social practices). The practice of science, in the way that it is done, is part of what actually happens—it is a historical phenomenon.

The historical aspect of scientific practice has presented certain kinds of problems, particularly in conjunction with the methodological aspect. One example will suffice:

10

The historical character of scientific practices as a particular institution within our society and similar societies receives some explicit treatment in the recent sociological development of "ethnomethodology." The result is a legitimization problem which is parallel to the classical "sociology of knowledge" problem, though in a more sophisticated vein. For to suppose that scientific accounts are simply what certain people say in accordance with the standards that govern their practices is to imply that all such accounts, including the very supposition in question (e.g., ethnomethodology), are ineluctably parochial in their content and outlook and therefore contrast with a simply factual account of what actually happens. But this result violates the methodological character of science, which requires that scientific accounts be factual accounts of what actually happens. Similarly, any stimulus-response or other causal approach to behavior will pose this kind of problem, since such accounts are simplified forms of historical explanation. In short, under existing treatments of the subject, the condition that scientific accounts be factual accounts of the real world is both a requirement and an impossibility.

On the whole, it appears that there is not now generally available any adequate treatment of reality and reality concepts or their connections to empirical science. From a diagnostic point of view, I should want to suggest that the failure to deal adequately with these topics either singly or jointly accounts in large part for the intellectual shambles in which current behavioral science finds itself, and I shall exhibit some part of the basis for taking this to be the case.

In reviewing the difficulties encountered in regard to the methodological, substantive, and historical connections between behavioral science and the real world, it becomes evident why these connections must be dealt with within a single, coherent formulation. It is apparent that where such coordination is not accomplished methodology, theory, and history inevitably become imperialistic, hence mutually destructive. Clearly, what is required for an intellectually responsible behavioral science is that methodology, substantive conceptualization, and historical accounts be complementary and mutually supportive. What we encounter in our current intellectual milieu is quite otherwise, namely

1. Methodological requirements (drawn from a reconstruction of physics) which (a) allow only degenerate cases (cause-effect) of historical accounts as scientific and leave genuinely historical accounts as unscientific (recall the Dray and Hempel controversy) and (b) make behavioral theory and research trivial or impossible except where, by luck or chance, physicists' (etc.) methods and productive behavioral methods coincide;

2. Substantive theories which (a) make historical accounts trivial or impossible and (b) make methodological requirements of any kind impossible, invalid, or epiphenomenal; and

3. Historical accounts (some simple forms of which are behavioral theories) which make both methodological requirements and substantive theories either historical accidents or historical necessities or both and therefore either trivial, invalid, or epiphenomenal.

The mutual destructiveness is publicly concealed largely by making the three into separate disciplines, keeping them in logic-tight compartments, and legitimizing the separation as a methodological requirement. It is in the practice and practitioners and consumers of 'behavioral science' that the destructive results are evident.

Moreover, it does not appear to be at all difficult to construct respectable historical and social-psychological accounts of how the present state of affairs has come about. To take one thread, for

12

example, and briefly: We may distinguish three ranges of facts, namely (a) the range of facts studied by physicists, (b) the range of facts studied by behavioral scientists, and (c) the range of facts comprising the practice of science by scientists. We next note that the range of facts (c) falls entirely within the range (b) and falls entirely outside the range (a). Thus, for physical science, the conduct of that science does not fall within the scope of its subject matter and so it is not something that physical theories could or should provide an account of. In contrast, the conduct of behavioral science or any other science is straightforwardly part of the subject matter of behavioral science; hence it is something which behavioral theories must give an account of if there is to be any substantively adequate general theory of behavior. Such an account of the facts of scientific behavior would have to be an adequate account of those facts and not merely an account which was not self-contradictory and in some vague sense "applied to" that behavior. Attempts at such accounts are what we have called "methodology" or "philosophy of science."

In this light it can be seen that although the separation of methodology from theory was proper and inevitable in the physical sciences, in the behavioral sciences it is preposterous and self-annihilating.

Now, a philosopher of science could hardly do otherwise than to preserve that separation, since without it he would be in an impossible position, for then there would be no philosophy of science (not of behavioral science, and not of the familiar kind) as a discipline distinct from the science itself. Since, in addition, the physical sciences are what influential philosophers of science universally use as their paradigm cases which form the anecdotal basis for their nonscientific theories of scientific behavior, it is entirely understandable that philosophical reconstructions of "the scientific method" should embody the separation of scientific methodology and scientific theory. Such reconstructions have always been used prescriptively by behavioral scientists as a social group, partly because the group is subject to pressure from the wider scientific community upon which it is parasitical and partly because the group, like any group, operates in a variety of ways to keep its members in line, and partly because no full-fledged alternative has been visible. Thus, we have that separation today, and its destructive consequences are pervasive and evident.

So much for the historical reconstruction. From the foregoing, it should be clear why it would seem that a viable behavioral science would require a different order of innovation than merely a new theory, a different methodology, or a novel historical approach, a different metaphysics, philosophy of science, philosophy of mind, etc. It is as much the divisions among these disciplines as their traditional contents which are at issue.

As I indicated above, my primary purpose is constructive rather than critical, just as it is scientific rather than philosophical. The historical, substantive, and methodological connections between behavioral science and the real world can be dealt with within behavioral science, in detail and coherently, by reference to a specific conceptual organization of four articulated basic concepts, namely, "reality," "person," "behavior," and "language."

In the present paper I shall be primarily concerned with one of these four concepts, namely, "reality," and with the most neglected of the three connections, the substantive one, between science and the real world. In Sections V and VI, I shall examine some of the ways in which reality concepts have entered into behavioral theories and behavioral theorizing and some additional and alternative ways in which it appears that they might do so in the future. That discussion is, naturally, limited by the fact that the systematic treatment of "person," "behavior," and "language" is accomplished in a subsequent paper and cannot be presupposed here.

14

II

A PRIMARY SYSTEMATIZATION
OF REALITY CONCEPTS

I REFERRED ABOVE to a conceptual organization of the articulated concept of "reality," "person," "behavior," and "language." The overall conceptual structure within which these four concepts are the principal constituents is designated as the Human Model or the Person Concept. The enterprise of elaborating the structure and using it in dealing systematically and effectively with the facts of behavior is designated as Descriptive Psychology. The overall organization depends on the separate articulation of each of the four primary concepts. Without that, we could get no further than the commonsense notions that people are a part of the real world, that they behave in various ways, and that verbal behavior is one such way. The technical conceptual formulation will preserve these notions, of course.

The articulation of the concept of "reality" is accomplished by reference to four basic reality concepts, namely, "object," "process," "event," and "state of affairs," and their further development.

By way of preliminary examination, we may note that these are not invented technical terms. Rather, they are already straightforwardly concepts of reality or the real world. A primary and paradigmatic use of these concepts is as the categories of "what there is." Thus, for example, one of the principal ways of formulating the claim that Z's are real is to say that they are a certain kind of object (e.g., a mental object, a mathematical object, an invisible physical object) or a certain kind of process (e.g., a mental process, a submicroscopic process, a learning process), etc.

Also, and by no means unrelated, the four reality concepts are observation concepts—we observe exemplars of each kind. To observe something on a given occasion is (at least) to find out something about it without on that occasion having to find out something else first (observation contrasts with inference). For example, I observe an object when I see an automobile, smell a fish, hear a bell, touch a person, or taste an apple. I observe a process when I hear the automobile coming down the road, feel the water turning warm, hear the music rising to a climactic pitch, or see the infant bouncing in his crib or working himself into a rage. I observe an event when I hear the motor stop, feel the wire snap, or see the flash in the sky. I observe a state of affairs when I hear that the singer is off-key, feel that the coat is threadbare, taste the difference between brand X and brand Y, or see that he is overjoyed or that they didn't understand, that the brass instrument is faulty, that the respiration rate has increased, etc.

What we observe is the real world. The fact that some exemplars of each of the four kinds of concept are observable provides one entree to the logical relations among these concepts. For without those relationships our observations would be as unrelated as the number 17, the color orange, and the Day of Judgment; and the very concept of "observation" would be lacking. The fact that our separate observations can be formulated as observations of a single world, i.e., the real world, requires that there be logical relationships among the concepts in terms of which our observations are made and our world described.

The general idea of there being such logical relationships is not a new one, of course. It was expressed by Kant in his Categories and Functions, and it appears in the current philosophical literature

16

under the conventional designation of "our conceptual scheme." What is novel in the present formulation is that the unification of "the real world" is accomplished explicitly and directly in terms of the reality concepts themselves by formulating them as elements in a calculational system. This contrasts with a unity which is merely implicit in our judgments but which can be argued for philosophically (Kant) or with a unity which is fully exhibited in a single structure (i.e., "our conceptual scheme").

With these preliminaries, let us turn to the reality concepts which form one major portion of the Person Concept. These concepts, which comprise a formal system of a certain, distinctive sort, are defined by their relationships to one another and not by any name relation or referring function vis-à-vis something external to the system. They are six in number, not four. "Object," "process," "event," and "state of affairs" are our primary categories for *what* there is. "Relation" (or "property," see below) is our major category for *how* things are or *what* sort of things there is. "Concept" is a status category by virtue of which the reality *concepts* have a place within the Person Concept.

The formal system of reality concepts is presented in Table 1 in the form of a set of transition rules, or transformations. What remains invariant under these transformations is real-world identity. What changes is the form of representation.

The state-of-affairs system is even neater and simpler than it appears in Table 1, since it could be compressed considerably into fewer and less redundant rules (for example, by stopping after Rule 7). The point at present, however, is to optimize its intelligibility in order to facilitate its explicit use. In this regard, certain remarks are called for in order that it not be grossly misunderstood. These remarks are directed toward questions concerning (1) the status of the system as a "formal" system, (2) the nature of the products of the system, (3) relationships and attributes, (4) the absence of

TABLE 1	*State-of-Affairs System Transition Rules*

1. A state of affairs is a totality of related objects and/or processes and/or events and/or states of affairs.
2. A process (or object or event or state of affairs) is a state of affairs which is a constituent of some other state of affairs.
3. An object is a state of affairs having other, related objects as immediate constituents. (An object divides into related, smaller objects.)
4. A process is a sequential change from one state of affairs to another.
5. A process is a state of affairs having other, related processes as immediate constituents. (A process divides into related, sequential or parallel, smaller processes.)
6. An event is a direct change from one state of affairs to another.
7. An event is a state of affairs having two states of affairs (i.e., "before" and "after") as constituents.
8. That a given state of affairs has a given relationship (e.g., succession, incompatibility, inclusion, common constituents, etc.) to a second state of affairs is a state of affairs.
8a. That a given object or process or event has a given relationship to another object or process or event is a state of affairs.
9. That a given object, process, event, or state of affairs is of a given kind is a state of affairs.
10. That an object or process begins is an event and that it ends is a different event.
10a. That an object or process occurs (begins and ends) is a state of affairs having three states of affairs ("before," "during," and "after") as constituents.

any reference to concepts, and (5) the relations of the system as such to the real world as such.

1. *In What Sense a "Formal System"?*

From the outset, it is important to avoid confusion and vacuous controversy over what it amounts to to say that the state-of-affairs system (SA system) is a formal or calculational system. I have in mind here the Element-Operation-Product conception of a formal system. In such a system a finite set of Elements and Operations are introduced explicitly. Operations are, by definition, performed on Elements (with or without restrictions on which is allowable with which), and every combination of Element and Operation has a result which is a Product. Every Product serves as a new Element. Finally, there is a distinctive notation for representing an element as an Element and a distinctive notation for representing an element as a Product (i.e., as an Element-Operation combination). For example, if we think of numbers as the elements in the arithmetic system, then "12" is a representation of a certain number as an Element, whereas "7 + 5" and "20 — 8" and "4 ×3" are ways of representing *the same* number as a Product. The preservation of numerical identity across changes in form of representation is the essence of arithmetic calculation, and it provides a familiar analogue for the preservation of real-world identity across changes in form of representation within the state-of-affairs system, hence the characterization of the latter as a "calculational system."

These several features distinguish the state-of-affairs system as a formal system, and nothing hinges on whether it is "really" a formal system in any narrower sense. For example, the utility of the formulation does not depend on giving explicit definitions of such expressions as "change," "occurrence," and "sequential." Nevertheless, since the Transition Rules do not obviously conform to the "Element-Operation-Product" format, some further explanation is called for.

To begin with, let us note that each Transition Rule consists of a left-hand element and a right-hand element connected by the word "is." It is these which correspond to Element, Product, and Operation, respectively.

The primary Transition Rules (1–7) are rules for reidentifying (or redescribing) something that is already identified (or described) as being an object, process, event, or state of affairs. (Rules 8–10 are heuristic and are intended to clarify the range of applicability of the concept of "state of affairs.") Every reidentification (Product) is an identification of that something as being an object, process, event, or state of affairs. Thus, the convertibility of Products into Elements is automatically guaranteed.

The primary cases of the use of the system are those in which the original description is given as a result of observation. However, since we are dealing now with the system as such and not yet with its use, it would be possible to specify explicitly four primitive Elements which would introduce our four reality concepts in a purely formal way. These Elements would be "object," "process," "event," and "state of affairs." The corresponding descriptions would be "Here is an object," "Here is a process," etc.

As to Operations, there in fact is one explicitly represented in the Transition Rules. This Operation, which we may call "Identity Coordination," is represented by the word "is."

It should be clear that the "is" which connects Elements and Product is to be understood as "is the same thing as" rather than "has the characteristic of." For example, a rose is the same thing as a specimen of a kind of flower, and a rose may have the characteristic of red, but a rose is not the same thing as red. The locution "the same thing as" is not used in the Transition Rules because it too readily suggests the traditional semantic distinction between meaning and reference and thereby invites the very question which discredits that distinction as being in any way fundamental, namely, "Well, *what* thing is it that *these* things are the same thing as?" Note that we have no tendency whatever to ask "But *what* number is it that '12', '20 — 8', '4 × 3', '7 + 5', etc., are the same as?" It does not appear that a language with Identity Coordination will have any deficiencies which need to be made good by a theory of

20

reference, and this will be of some significance at a later time in dealing with the problem of what it is that behavioral science is *about*.

Given the single Operation of Identity Coordination, the kind of Product that is generated is a function of the kind of Element one begins with. (Compare: Given the single Operation of Addition, the kind of Sum that is generated is a function of the numbers one begins with.) This much is clear-cut.

However, on the face of it there is some ground for uneasiness in the fact that one may begin with the same Element and Operation and generate different Products. For example, "process" is transformed by Rule 4 into "a sequential change from one state of affairs to another," hence (by Rule 1) into a sequential change in a state of affairs; but it is also transformed by Rule 5 into "a state of affairs having other, related processes as immediate constituents." However, no contradictions are introduced in this way. What follows is that this sequential change in a state of affairs is the same thing as a state of affairs having related processes as immediate constituents. That is, the state of affairs which encompasses the sequential change is the state of affairs which has the sequentially related process as constituents. Both of the transitions given by Rules 4 and 5 are essential to the concept of "process," and neither the meaning nor the logical role of that concept is fully given by any single Transition Rule.

The Transition Rules provide only the basic articulation of the reality concepts. For this purpose, simple intelligibility is crucial. And it does not appear that any of the Transition Rules are difficult to understand. On the other hand, since the answer to such a question as "What is a process?" is distributed across the various Transition Rules, that answer is given only implicitly by the Transition Rules. It is the extended systematization developed in Section III which provides a direct answer: Given the formulation there of "Process description" or "Process representation," we may then say "A process is anything that exemplifies a Process representation." In the Process representation, the compatibility and complementarity of Rule 4 and Rule 5 is exhibited.

2a. *Permissive Transitions and Elaborations of Descriptions*

Given the characterization of something as an object or process or event or state of affairs, no redescription at all is required by the SA system. In this sense, each of the Transition Rules is entirely permissive rather than obligatory.

Taken collectively, however, the Transition Rules may be characterized as strongly, but conditionally, obligatory. The condition is that one's observations be intelligible. If no transitions were accomplished, then it would seem at first glance that all descriptions would be bare cases of "Here is a case of X." Under these conditions, it would be impossible to accomplish even the first move that William James attributed to the normal infant, namely, "Thingumbob *again*," for that would be to say that what I observe now is *the same thing as* what I observed then. But under these conditions even "Here is an X" would be entirely vacuous, for without being able to reidentify the same X we could have no concepts of particular things that would qualify as an X. In this sense, the Transition Rules are, collectively, obligatory. This notion is developed further in the discussion of "Chronological description" in Section III.

There is a second and very different respect in which we may speak of permissive and obligatory in connection with the Transition Rules. That is in regard to whether a redescription, given in accordance with a Transition Rule, replaces the original description or, alternatively, enriches or elaborates it.

Either alternative is always possible, so that the rules are permissive rather than obligatory in this sense also. It does appear, however, that in most cases our redescriptions are used to elaborate rather than to replace. Thus, for example, when a nation is said to be an object (Gruner, 1969) which is a state of affairs having as constituents smaller objects (persons) standing in certain (political) relationships, we do not replace the description of something as a nation with a description of something as that state of affairs. Instead, we keep both by saying that *that* nation is *that* state of affairs. The State-of-Affairs description elaborates the description of the nation as an object, and does not replace it.

For a simple and familiar example of the enrichment of description by successive elaborations, we may turn once more to the nursery:

> This is the house that Jack built.
> This is the table that stood in the house that Jack built.
> This is the cheese that lay on the table that stood in the house that Jack built.
> This is the horse that kicked the dog that chased the cat that ate the rat that nibbled the cheese that lay on the table that stood in the house that Jack built.

And compare:

(1). This is the object that's part of the object that's part of the object that Jack observed.

(2). This is the object that's part of the state of affairs that's the same as the process that ended in the event that introduced the state of affairs that Jack observed.

The latter descriptive formula should have a familiar ring to it in spite of the prosaic idiom. It resembles in form our "theoretical" scientific "explanations" of observed states of affairs. Indeed, in that particular formula the "object" mentioned would equally well fit a "cognitive structure" in a calculational account of problem solving (the latter being the observed state of affairs) or a "physiological structure" in a physiological account of "the same" observed result. But, then, of course, all of us in the various sciences are, no less than the historians, engaged in the study of "what actually happens."

2b. *Descriptions and Descriptive Formulas*

It should be clear from the foregoing example that the products of the SA system are not particular descriptions of the real world, but rather logical formulas (forms, formats, schemas, paradigms) for such descriptions. Systematic descriptions or particular descriptions are generated when the objects, processes, events, states of affairs, and relationships which appear in a given reality formula are specified as to *kind* (see Rule 9) or identified as *which*.

It should also be clear that the range of reality formulas generated by the SA system is infinite in variety and not merely in number. For example, the difference between the formulas exemplified above by (1) "This is the object . . . " and (2) "This is the object . . . " is quite comparable to the structural difference between

(3) $$X+Y+Z+Q$$

(4) $$X/(Y+Z)+Q$$

By way of elaboration on the complexity and variety which is possible, let us consider here a general kind of reidentification procedure which is of some independent interest, scientifically. We begin with the identification of an observed object, process, event, or state of affairs, and let us suppose that in a particular case it is an object (e.g., as in "This is the object . . . " in (2), above). The reidentification then consists of an SA-system formula (i.e., one which conforms to the Transition Rules) involving some number of objects, processes, events, or states of affairs, where these latter are defined by their relationship to the object (etc.) which is observed—as in (1) and (2), above. The latter are thereby *hypothetical* objects, processes, etc. It is by reference to such hypotheticals that much of our "explaining" has been done.

Note that the introduction of hypothetical objects, processes, etc., which are defined by their relationship to what is observed is, in important respects, the SA-system analogue of an ordinary algebraic equation such as

(2a) $$12 = x/(y+2)+Q$$

(2b) $$12 = x + [(y + (2 + Q)]$$
(2c) $$12 = (x/y)/(2-Q)$$

What is observed corresponds to the constant in these equations. Just as the right-hand side of each of these equations specifies something that the constant is the same as, so our hypothetical reality formulas specify something that our observed object (process, etc.) is the same as.

Two points are worth noting here. First, the entire equation will be uninformative if the right-hand side is not formulated in product notation (i.e., as an Element-Operation combination). In that case, we would have something like (2d).

(2d) $$12 = x$$

The corresponding SA-system equation would be the equivalent of a homunculus explanation, i.e., what is observed would simply be set in a one-to-one relation to what is hypothesized. Second, since there are only variables on the right-hand side, there is no constraint

25

on what sort of algebraic expression appears on the right side except the formal constraints governing well-formed algebraic expressions. Likewise, in the SA-system equation, since there are only hypotheticals on the right-hand side, there is no constraint on what sort of reality formula appears on the right-hand side except the Transition Rules of the SA-system. We may invent or introduce *any* collections of objects, processes, events, and/or affairs as the hypothetical antecedents, correlates, or consequences of our observed object (process, etc.) so long as we introduce them *as* antecedents, correlates, or consequences.

To put it more dramatically, from each single observation we make, we can construct a hypothetical reidentification formula so complex and extensive as to represent the past, present, and future history of the universe. Thus, one further parallel between ordinary algebraic calculation and SA-system calculation: In general, a single formula such as (2a), (2b), or (2c) is of no consequence, because there are too many variables. However, when some number of equations can be considered simultaneously we can "solve" the equations in order to decide whether they are compatible, i.e., whether there are determinate values or less-complex equations which must be satisfied if all the equations are to hold simultaneously. Likewise, the reality formulas which we value are those which reduce to a single formula which is compatible with all our observations. We have no way of "solving" for this result, but we are able to decide.

In this vein, then, the task of giving an empirical account of the real world (this world, the world we observe, as contrasted with merely possible worlds) is the task of inventing, updating, and maintaining a world formula within which we can fit, as constituents, the more limited reality formulas with which we represent what we observed and the fact of our having observed it in the way we did. As we shall see (e.g., Sections III and VI), to represent empiricism in this way is to provide the basis for a new view of the task and character of the various sciences, and particularly behavioral science.

3. Relationships and Attributes

In the Transition Rules, mention is made both of (a) something being related to something and (b) something being of a certain kind. The adoption of this way of talking is in the interest of clarity and intelligibility. In fact both cases can be accommodated by the single expression "attribute." As defined by Carnap (*Introduction to Symbolic Logic*), an attribute is an n-place relation, where n may equal $1, 2, \ldots, K$. A 1-place relation is a property, and if something has the property P, then it is of kind P. For n greater than 1, an n-place attribute is a relationship among n elements.

4. What Is the Status of Concepts?

There is a conspicuous omission in the Transition Rules. Of the six concepts which were identified as the fundamental reality concepts, the Transition Rules mention five. The sixth, namely, "concept," is not mentioned at all. How, then, does "concept" enter the picture at all?

The answer is simple, but only provisionally satisfactory. That is that the entire SA system is a single concept, or conceptual organization, and it involves not objects, processes, etc., but rather the *concepts* "object," "process," "event," "state of affairs," and "relationship." Moreover, the distinguishable kinds of each of these, which must come into the picture in going from descriptive formulas to descriptions, all correspond to different concepts.

The answer is only provisionally satisfactory because it raises a new question about the status of "concept." If the entire SA system is a single concept, then where, in what possible context, is there a place for concepts and what is their place there? Once again, the full answer requires the entire Person Concept.

A brief answer here is that "concept" is not to be reified as a kind of something. A concept is not an object or process, etc., so it is not something we are going to encounter or observe. Rather, "concept" is a logical derivative from the more complex "P uses concept X" or "P acts on concept X." So the answer to "Where do concepts have a place?" is "Concepts have a place in behavior, because the concept 'concept' has a place in the concept 'behavior'." The clarification of what that place is must be given by the detailed articulation of the concept of behavior within the Person Concept. A crucial feature of that articulation is to dissolve the apparent paradox of saying that the general category of "concept" has a place in the particular concept of behavior. These considerations have been dealt with at some length elsewhere (Ossorio, 1966a, 1969a, 1969b). Suffice it to say that in a reflexive conceptual structure such "paradoxes" are neither unusual nor paradoxical.

5. The State-of-Affairs System and the Real World

The State-of-Affairs System, as a conceptual system, is an articulation of the concept of "reality" as a methodological status concept. (Recall the methodological connection referred to initially between behavioral science and the real world.) We could have said "science is realistic" and been no less realistic, i.e., in accordance with reality constraints, than in saying, as we did, "science is empirical." The latter happens to be traditional. The concept of "the real world" is the concept of a historical particular, and it is as a historical particular which exemplifies certain specifiable regularities that the real world is what any given science is *about*. (Recall the substantive connection between behavioral science and the real world.) The formulation of the state-of-affairs system permits us to examine some of the relations between the two.

For this purpose (and for other purposes later on), there are two among the various procedures for generating reality formulas which will be of special interest. These are designated as *composition* with respect to objects, processes, events, and states of affairs and *decomposition* with respect to objects, processes, and states of affairs.

Both composition and decomposition involve part-whole relationships and both involve progressive enrichment, or elaboration, from some starting point (generally speaking, starting from what is established by observation). In decomposition, a single something (which may be an object or process or state of affairs) is redescribed as a set of related constituents of the same sort. That is, objects decompose into other, related objects (Rule 3); processes decompose into other, related processes (Rule 5); and states of affairs decompose into other, related states of affairs (Rule 1). The converse is the case in composition. That is, related sets of objects are redescribed as a state of affairs which is the same as a new, single object (Rules 8a, 1); sets of related processes are composed into a new, single process (Rules 8a, 1, 5); and sets of related states of affairs are composed into a new, single state of affairs (Rules 8, 1). And, since processes can be composed, so can events (Rule 10). Finally, since Rules 1, 3, and 5 are recursive, composition and decomposition can be carried on indefinitely.

It is against the background of the unlimited possibility of composition and decomposition that certain limiting cases take on intelligibility and significance. The following are among the most familiar and important limiting cases:

LC-I   The state of affairs which includes all other states of affairs (i.e., "the real world").

LC-II   A type of object that is not a state of affairs (i.e., it has no constituents, and so is an ultimate object—a "basic building block").

LC-III   A type of process that is not a state of affairs (i.e., it has no constituents, hence no beginning that is distinct from its end, hence is the effective equivalent of an event). (Perhaps most "literally" it would be a unit class of events. Note also that a "mental mechanism" will be of this sort unless it is a process which has constituents of this sort.)

LC-IV   A type of process that is a state of affairs but has no process constituents (i.e., is the effective equivalent of an object during a period in which the object undergoes no change—cf. molecular processes at "absolute zero temperature").

The significance of the limiting cases is that they are ways of putting an end to the composition (LC-I) and decomposition (LC-II, III, IV) of the primitive reality concepts. The result of introducing limiting cases is a type of formula which is suitable for representing a single, boundaryless, historical particular of indefinite extent or a single, unbounded set of historical particulars. In either case, we have a "world formula," which is the kind of thing that "our conceptual scheme" is. There are several significant aspects of this state of affairs.

(a) The "ultimate" objects or processes achieved by LC-II or LC-III cannot be specified merely *as* ultimate. They must be identified as being of one general sort or another (without this specification we would have only empty formulas, not descriptions). And what distinguishes one sort of object or process from another is the kinds of relationships it can enter into. Thus, the kind of object or process that is specified here will set limits to the kinds of relationships that such objects could enter into. Correspondingly, the states of affairs which could obtain in a world which simply consisted of such objects and their by-definition composites would be limited. So also would the totality of such states of affairs be limited, in range if not in number. In short, the choice of ultimate object or process sets limits to the kind of "world" which corresponds to such representation.

In point of fact, the situation is somewhat more complex. Ultimate objects or processes need not be of just a single kind. They may simply be the various primitive kinds of object or process defined by a conceptual system. Any one of a large variety of conceptual systems can be used thus in selecting ultimate constituents. Each selection determines a kind of "world." Some selections are more familiar than others and some are often taken to be more general, more fundamental, or more real than others. Thus, we speak not only of "the art world," "the world of fashion," "the baseball world," and "the academic world," but also of "the physical world," "the biological world," and "the world of nature."

Not only is any particular limit setting arbitrary in that its choice cannot be certified as being simply a reflection of how the world is, but also the restriction of one's choice to a single limit setting (whether in terms of a single kind of ultimate or a single conceptual system) is a further arbitrary choice, and it is one which can obviously be rejected. There is no reason why different kinds of objects should not be identified as ultimate relative to a certain range of possible facts (states of affairs). Indeed, this is what the hard facts of the matter have always required of us in order to span the entire range of facts with which we are acquainted. In this regard, the traditional scientific ideologies phrased in terms of "determinism" and "reductionism" are not merely nonempirical, but, one might say, actively antiempirical. To be sure, the commitment to such postures is usually presented with engaging candor as an article of faith, but it is not clear that a scientific respect for fact leaves room for theological practice even in this vestigial form.

The arbitrariness of limit setting is not restricted to the kind of object or process, etc., which is selected as ultimate. It also appears in the choice of which of the reality concepts is used in specifying the ultimate units and the nature of the totality. The mutual convertibility of the basic reality concepts as forms of representation has the consequence that "the real world" may equally well be conceived as (1) an all-encompassing state of affairs (LC-I), (2) an all-encompassing object, (3) an all-encompassing process, or (4) an all-encompassing succession of events. Historically, each of these conceptions of "what there is" has had its proponents; and it has long been recognized that any of them will do the job, so that "you pays your money and you takes your choice."

The formulation of the SA system renders these historical facts entirely intelligible and unsurprising. However, it provides no motivation toward seeing it as a matter of paying your money and taking your choice. Taking that view would be comparable to taking the view that since every integer can be expressed either as a sum or a difference or a product or a quotient, when it comes to dealing with numbers you pay your money and take your choice among addition, subtraction, multiplication, and division. But the function of arithmetic operations is not to provide a catalogue of "what there is" in the way of integers. Their prime function is to generate numbers from numbers and connect numbers to numbers, and that function has a human value when the numbers which are connected or generated correspond to some kind of knowledge on our parts. Likewise, the primary function of the reality concepts is not to provide us with a catalogue of "what there is" in the world. Rather it is to connect representations to representations or to generate represen-

32

tations from representations, and that has some human value when those representations correspond to what we observe or what we are otherwise capable of knowing about the world. We are not merely spectators of the world, but actors in it as well, and as actors we need more than a taxonomy of "what there is."

I shall later want to suggest that the only "world" which does not represent an arbitrary, a priori limitation on possible states of affairs and which, therefore, includes all the other "worlds" and qualifies as simply "the real world" (LC-I) is the one that would be most naturally called "the behavioral world," or "the human world," and that is the one which is codified in the Human Model, or Person Concept. This notion will, of course, have a bearing on the issue of whether there is a problem of "foundations" for behavioral science.

(b) The concept of "reality" corresponds to the SA system as such, hence is more fundamental than the various concepts of "the real world" which are derived from it via the limiting cases and choices of ultimates. Since such limits and choices are entirely arbitrary with respect to the SA system as such, they must be introduced extraneously. And they are—by persons. Every conception, observation, or description of "the real world" or any of its parts or aspects is someone's conception, observation, or description. Hence there is a person with respect to whom it has the methodological status of *my* conception, observation, or description. That is a conceptual and methodological necessity, not a matter of phenomenology. (Recall that the SA system is a fragment of the more complex logical structure of the Person Concept, which includes persons, behavior, and language as well. The "my" here is part of what requires the reflexive structure referred to above in commenting on the place of "concept" within the Person Concept.)

(c) In traditional scientific theorizing, the substantive concept of a theory is categorically distinct from the methodological principles by reference to which its standing within the social institution

33

of its particular science is appraised. This gives *all* such theories a distinctive cast which might be characterized as a "pictorial," or "entity," perspective. That is, the primary concern is with objects (or "structures") and processes ("deterministic" causal processes) via LC-II, III, and IV.

The relation between the separation of methodology and the "pictorial" quality may be clarified by reference to the familiar example of actual pictures. A picture (or description), e.g., of a man and a dog walking in front of a house, can portray certain objects, processes, events, and states of affairs. What it cannot portray is any state of affairs which constitutes its own methodological status. For example, it cannot portray the fact that it *is* a picture or the fact that it is a picture *of* a man and a dog walking in front of a house. Nor can it portray any instructions or prescriptions or standards concerning what one could sensibly do with a picture. Nor can it portray any definition or instruction as to what a picture is and is not. It is only because these fundamentals are already taken care of in other ways than with pictures that there are such things as pictures and that they have the value that they do. Likewise, it is only because considerations of methodological status are already taken care of in other ways than by traditional scientific theories that there are such things as traditional scientific theories and that they have the value and standing that they do in our real world. And methodological principles have the form of facts (states of affairs), not objects or processes.

In contrast to traditional theorizing, the Person Concept contains principles of scientific methodology as a substantive special case; and this, too, gives it a distinctive cast which might be characterized as a "methodological," or "factual" perspective. That is, the primary conceptual concern is with facts, or states of affairs, via LC-I. It is because it deals principally and essentially with states of affairs rather than simply with objects or processes that the Person

34

Concept has no difficulty in principle with methodological facts or with the fact that they *are* methodological facts. These are behavioral facts.

It should not be surprising, therefore, that in the Person Concept the pre-empirical conceptualization of empiricism should have a distinctive cast also and that it contrasts with the empiricism which reflects the pictorial perspective. This contrast is reflected in the adoption of "reality" and "the real world" as the basic form of empiricism in the two approaches, respectively.

From the pictorial perspective on empiricism, what distinguishes the real world from merely possible worlds is that certain descriptions ("pictures") are applicable to what we observe, and these descriptions contrast with other descriptions which do not apply to what we observe but which might have applied and would apply in some possible worlds.

From the methodological perspective, what distinguishes reality from mere possibility is that we are (in fact) limited in what we can and can't do in just those ways in which we are (in fact) limited, and not in any of the other ways in which we might possibly have been limited.

As the boundary condition on our possible behaviors, reality in no way *resembles* the scenes we see as we look around us (nor yet a submicroscopic or cosmic picture thereof). This is because it is categorically different from the latter, hence not comparable in the usual way as to similarity or difference. In a similar and more familiar vein, the English language does not resemble the English sentences that we speak (nor does chess resemble pawn moves or checkmates), because the language and the sentences are categorically different. It would be quite in keeping with our hypothetico-deductive custom to say that the sentences are the observable manifestations of the language (or linguistic competence). But neither the fact (cf. Rules 8a, 10a) that the "sentences" are being "uttered" or that the "sounds" are being "emitted" is in any way more "observable" than the fact that it is "English" that is being "spoken." Our access to the English language is by observation, not inference.

And it may be worth commenting that the methodological formulation cannot be reduced to the previous case (the pictorial formulation) by exhibiting a description of our behavioral capabilities and limitations (which change over time, of course, sometimes in part as a result of just such efforts) and saying that this is just one of the descriptions which is applicable to the real world. (This is, of course, old-fashioned naturalism applied to behavior.) The boundary condition would reappear in the form of the limitations on how we were able to act on *that* description.

Thus, in place of the pictorially motivated traditional question "Is the description (the predictive one) *true* (or false) and is the other description (the theoretical one) *true* (or false)?" we may offer a new formula for scientific empiricism—"Has it been demonstrated that *as a matter of fact there is a point in talking that way?*" This formula is applicable whether the talk in question is (a) an observation report, (b) a "theoretical" description of what is observed, (c) a classically "methodological" statement to the effect, e.g., that a theoretical description has been "confirmed" or that it has been "operationalized," or (d) a modest statement to the effect that as a matter of fact there is a point in talking a certain way (or in not talking that way).

I have indicated above that our nonscientific theories of scientific behavior are deficient in that they are (in fact) unable to provide an adequate account of the sense in which scientific theories either (a) are empirical or (b) are factual accounts of the real world. From this, one might well conclude that as a matter of fact there is a point in not talking that way One of the advantages of the behavioral approach is that its empirical formula creates no mysteries and leaves no problems of this sort.

It is not to be supposed that the question "Has it been demonstrated that as a matter of fact there is a point in talking that way?" reflects the recently fashionable disparagement of language (as being *mere* "verbal behavior" in an S-R sense) or any general skepticism regarding it. On the contrary, an adequate formulation of language as a form of behavior is one of the indispensable conceptual units within the Person Concept. Thus, the question is asked with the expectation that it could commonly be answered in the affirmative. The phrase "talking that way" directs our attention to the necessity for a technically detailed, systematic representation of what it is that we can say or do say in talking scientifically about the real world. For any given scientific statement, we should want a systematic representation of what information is carried and what commitment is being made by "talking that way." (This is part of the scientific study of verbal behavior in general, not a merely ad hoc treatment of scientific verbal behavior.) The extended systematization of reality concepts presented in the following section may be used as a technical resource in this way. As a merely technical resource, it is independent of the contrast between the pictorial and the factual perspectives on empiricism and can be used in either way.

III

THE REPRESENTATION
OF "WHAT ACTUALLY HAPPENS"

THE CONCEPTS of "reality" and "the real world" were presented above as being the substantive correlatives of our use of the formal conceptual system delineated by means of the Transition Rules (the SA system) of Table 1. This system defines the concepts of "object," "process," "event," "state of affairs," and "relationship" by reference to one another. It brings together explanatory, methodological, and observational facts and concepts within a single conceptual system, and in this way provides one of the conceptual anchors for a science of behavior.

What the basic Transition Rules do not do explicitly is to provide procedures for distinguishing kinds of object, process, event, and state of affairs or for distinguishing historical particulars of these sorts. For example, since the rules deal with the general concept of a process, they apply to all processes, and so they do not serve to distinguish one process from another. But distinguishing one object, process, etc., from another is essential to the behavior which is our subject matter; and it is no less essential to the behavior of studying that subject matter scientifically. Thus, our reality concepts must be articulated at a new level of detail in order to serve a technical function in our scientific procedures. As we shall see, the resources for doing so are inherent in the Transition Rules.

What is required, then, is a systematic specification of the ways in which one object (or process, etc.) may resemble another or differ from another. Such a specification would amount to a parametric analysis of the reality categories of "object," "process," "event," "state of affairs," and "real world." What is required beyond this is a systematically related set of representational formats within which such specifications can be given.

The result of pursuing these requirements is a set of eight articulated representational formats. Five of these correspond directly to the four reality categories noted above; the remaining three are important derivative cases. Since these eight formats are systematically related to one another along the lines laid down by the Transition Rules, they are correspondingly recursive and convertible into one another, so that the entire set constitutes a single resource for representing the real world or any part or aspect thereof.

The representational formats provide the public, observable correlatives of the corresponding reality concepts, just as mathematical symbols provide the public, observable correlatives of mathematical concepts. And, as is the case with mathematical notation, these forms of representation may be considered either (1) as a systematic alternative to linguistic representation or (2) as being essentially linguistic, but having certain technical advantages over discursive sorts of presentation. This contrast is considered further below in connection with "State-of-Affairs description."

Thus, the representational formats are referred to variously as forms of representation, forms of description, or types of (conceptual-factual) analysis. The remainder of this section is devoted to the delineation of (a) Process description, (b) Object description, (c) Configuration description, (d) Chronological description, (e) Means-Ends description, (f) Task analysis, (g) Event description, and (h) State-of-Affairs description. As it happens the strategic entree to this range of descriptive formulas is in the middle (in point of complexity), with Process and Object descriptions. This is because of the strategic character of the composition and decomposition of Object and Process representations.

A. Process Description

The technical concept of a Process description is arrived at by specifying a basic descriptive unit which is recursive (hence can be composed and decomposed) and then specifying how the results of the recursive use may be tied together in a single logical structure. The primary basis for the technical elaboration is, as might be expected, Rule 4 and Rule 5.

Rule 4. A process is a sequential change from one state of affairs to another.

Rule 5. A process is a state of affairs which has as immediate constituents other, related processes. (A process divides into smaller, related (sequentially or parallel) processes.)

What is involved in the notion of "sequential" here is that the change in question from some state of affairs, A, to another one, B, consists of at least two successive changes, i.e., A-Q and Q-B. The interposition of Q is what carries the implication that, unlike an event, a process has duration. Then, since A-Q and Q-B are themselves processes, by Rule 5, each has duration and each consists of sequential changes, A-X, X-Q and Q-Y, Y-B. And so on. Since the division may be continued indefinitely and every such division may be divided indefinitely and this progression may be continued indefinitely, the limiting case will be the equivalent of all the non-terminating decimals, hence will correspond to a currently acceptable mathematical definition of "continuous" process. Thus, in the present formulation the notion of a discrete process given by Rule 4 and Rule 5 is the fundamental process concept and the continuous process formula is a generally dispensable derivative.

The gross structure of a Process description, i.e., "Name" and "Description" (see Table 2), reflects the relation of Rule 4 to Rule 5. We report the occurrence of a given process, A-B, by giving as its systematic "Name" an *identifying* description, usually of the normal discursive sort, e.g., "He shot the bear with a revolver." In representing "Name" as having occurred, we might then appeal immediately to LC-III or LC-IV and deny that any further "Description" applies (at some point we have to do this, except possibly with a continuous process); but normally we are committed to at least one sequential breakdown, A-Q, Q-B, which was not specified by "Name" per se. For example, "Well, he pointed the gun (A-Q) and pulled the trigger (Q-B)." Methodologically, we are back at the starting point; for A-Q has now been identified by a new "Name" as a process which has occurred, and so has Q-B. Either we now appeal to LC-III or LC-IV or we provide a new "Description" for A-Q and so on. In this way the SA-system formulation directly codifies the fact of our being able to give observational reports of just those processes which we are in a position to report, i.e., those which we can establish by observation as having occurred. This contrasts with the physicalistic-inferential view that our observations of processes represent inferences drawn from cues provided by the occurrence of theoretically describable continuous physical processes.

But "Name" and "Description" are merely the gross structural divisions of Process descriptions. To reach a technically effective level of detail, the Basic Process Unit (BPU) shown in Table 2 is proposed

In the Basic Process Unit each Option within a given stage is a constituent process with respect to P-NameA. Thus, it is the Stage-Option structure which codifies the recursiveness of the Transition Rules within the BPU. Decomposition can proceed in-

TABLE 2	*Basic Process Unit (BPU)*

P-NameA: The process "Name" of process A.

P-DescriptionA: The "Description" of A. It specifies:

I. P-Paradigms: The major varieties of P-NameA. This is a technical option. If only one paradigm exists, it will be the same as P-NameA. For each paradigm, the following is specified:

(a) Stages I-K: These are "Names" of subprocesses within A. They are systematically specified, e.g., as P-NameA11, P-NameA12, . . . , P-Name-A1K for Paradigm 1. For each stage, specify:

(1) Options 1-N: These are the various exemplars of the process (stage) in question. That is, these are the various ways in which that process could happen. Each Option is systematically indexed as P-NameA111, P-Name-A112, . . . , P-NameA11N. Each of these can now be expanded (decomposed) on the model of P-NameA.

(b) Individuals

(c) Elements

(d) Eligibilities

(e) Contingencies

(f) Versions

definitely by generating a BPU representation of any Option in P-NameA, then doing the same for any Option within *that* BPU, and so on. Composition is accomplished by identifying P-NameA with some Option within a more extensive process, say, P-NameQ.

Then P-NameA is *the same process as,* say, P-NameQ135. And so on.

In contrast, Individuals, Elements, Eligibilities, and Contingencies are designed to codify the state-of-affairs structure of the process P-NameA. By Rule 5, a process is a state of affairs that has related processes as immediate constituents. That state of affairs may also have other constituents. It will have event constituents, if only by virtue of Rule 10; and it will have state-of-affairs constituents, if only by virtue of Rule 10a. The major case of interest will involve object constituents. These must, then, be of certain kinds and stand in certain relations to one another in order that they should be the same thing as the state of affairs, which, after all, is already defined by reference to the process (Rules 1, 8a, 9).

Since the process P-NameA divides without remainder into constituent processes, the object constituents of that state of affairs (which might be systematically designated as PSA-NameA) would, in our ordinary way of talking, be constituents of that process and of some subprocess. "Element" provides a logical category within the concept of "process" which may be filled by an object or structure.

For example, if P-NameA is "He shot the bear with a revolver," a set of subprocesses would be (1) he raised the revolver with his hand; (2) he pointed the revolver at the bear; (3) he pulled the trigger of the revolver; and (4) the bullet shot out, (5) fatally wounding the bear. These would be Stages. Among the object constituents of the process P-NameA would be (a) the man, (b) his hand, (c) the revolver, (d) the trigger, (e) the bullet, and (f) the bear. These would be Elements.

Certain relationships do hold among these Elements. For example, "raised the revolver with his hand" refers to a relational structure (a state of affairs) involving (at least) the man, the hand, and the revolver. It is the sequential changes in this relational struc-

43

ture which is the same thing as the process. Thus, "He raised the revolver with his hand" is the identifying description (Name) for both a process (P-NameA1) and a state of affairs (PSA-NameA1) which is a constituent of a larger state of affairs (PSA-NameA). And there is a parallel treatment of "He pointed the revolver at the bear."

Given such examples of how "the same thing" can be described as a process, a relationship, and a state of affairs, we see some of the ambiguity which is systematically present in most scientific and nonscientific discourse and which calls for systematic answers to the question "What did he say?"

In this example there are some relationships which are not given by Process descriptions. For example, the trigger is *part of* the revolver, and it is a specific part. That relationship has no corresponding Process description unless we employ LC-IV, but it is part of that state of affairs (PSA-NameA1). Without that relationship there would be no such thing as shooting the bear with *that* revolver by pulling *that* trigger.

In general, then, the process Element provides the way to represent an "ingredient" *as such* of a process, and it is most pertinent when the ingredient is an object or structure. Ingredients have to be combined in certain ways, and the specification of what those ways are is given by the detailed (as much as needed) articulation of the state of affairs PSA-NameA in terms of constituent states of affairs. What is not yet specified is how many distinct individuals are required for the process and which of these individuals is eligible to participate in the process as which Elements. Thus, we have the additional logical categories of Individual and Eligibility in order to specify the state-of-affairs structure of a process. Individuals are specified in such a way (e.g., with numbers, names, letters, symbols) that they can be identified *as* individuals when that is needed.

In football, for example, we might distinguish 37 Elements, of which 22 are individually distinguished as the players of the various "positions." Among the 22 collectively, there is a wide variety of actions and practices which are the process constituents of the behavioral process (the social practice) of playing a football game. At the same time, the logical structure of that process is given in large part by the clear-cut constraints as to which of the 22 is eligible to do any particular one of those things, e.g., catch a pass, and under what circumstances. The latter notion brings us to the category of Contingency.

Within a given BPU, Contingencies provide further restrictions (given a specification of Name, Paradigm, Stages, Options, Elements, Individuals, and Eligibilities) as to what can occur and still be a case of P-NameA. Or else they are a factual constraint which merely summarize the statistics concerning the likelihood that a given Version (see below) of P-NameA would actually happen. Contingency specifications fall into two general classes, i.e., attribution constraints and co-occurrence constraints. What is contingent is the occurrence of a given component process (Stage-Option), and what it is contingent upon is either or both (1) given Elements having given characteristics or given relationships to other Elements (recall the trigger as *part of* the revolver) or (2) the occurrence of one or more other designated process components. The contingencies are states of affairs.

Examples of the first sort (attribution constraints) would include such specifications as (a) in a football game, the quarterback is a human being; the goalposts are not; (b) in a "double-bind" interaction, the Victim must be strongly motivated to understand the Binder; and (c) the fuel for our nonpolluting engine must be lacking in lead-compound additives.

With respect to co-occurrence constraints, it should be kept in mind that a component process of P-NameA can be identified and described independently of P-NameA, and the fact that it some-

45

times occurs as part of an instance of P-NameA does not imply that whenever it occurs it is part of an instance of P-NameA (nor, of course, that it occurs whenever an instance of P-NameA occurs). Thus, for example, if the gross sequential structure of "Dining" (P-NameA) is given by (a) preparation, (b) serving, (c) eating, and (d) cleaning up, then a co-occurrence constraint is given by saying that whatever is prepared is also served and also eaten. That is to say that, for example, although cabbages, apples, and steak are all eligible to be what is prepared or eaten or served, if it is apples that are prepared, then it is apples and not cabbages or steak that are eaten; conversely, if it is steak that is eaten, then it was steak and not cabbages or apples that was prepared. This contingency statement rules out such sequences as (a) preparing apples, (b) serving steak, and (c) eating cabbage. Note that co-occurrence constraints are not per se temporal constraints—a given occurrence may be expressed as contingent upon a later or concurrent occurrence no less than upon an earlier occurrence.

When the BPU is used recursively, more complex formulas are the result. The structure of such formulas is given (a) necessarily by the pattern of recursion, since every recursive use of the BPU decomposes some particular constituent process, hence has a definite place in the BPU from which the new BPU was generated; (b) generally also by Contingencies, which may connect Elements at any locations in the structure or to states of affairs external to the process in question; and (c) among such Contingencies are those which extend the Eligibilities of particular Individuals across the lines of recursion.

The concept of Version is, one might say, a way of representing the net results of the structural constraints on P-NameA which are provided by Paradigms, Stages, Options, Elements, Individuals, Eligibilities, and Contingencies. The net result of these constraints is to delimit the possible cases of P-NameA. A version of P-NameA is simply one of the possible cases of P-NameA. Since P-NameA is a process, its exemplars will be occurrences of processes. Thus, a version of P-NameA is one of the ways that P-NameA could occur on a given occasion. Conversely, the occurrence of P-NameA on a given occasion is the same thing as the occurrence of some one of its versions on that occasion. Since different versions of the same process, P-NameA, need not resemble one another in any way other than their being alternative versions, the empirical study of processes takes on a certain kind of complexity. It is significant, for example, that our social practice of studying behavioral processes experimentally involves examining particular versions of P-NameA and expressing the findings as discoveries about P-NameA per se, and this move is essential to the customary form of that practice. And it raises questions which cannot be dealt with here. The different versions of P-NameA may be given by a list or by a formula for generating them.

Consider now a simple example of the analysis of a social process by a sociologist (Garfinkel, 1967). The process, or practice, in question is the "degradation ceremony." A classic example of such a ceremony is the case of a noncommissioned officer who has been convicted of a grave breach of military discipline; he is marched out before the assembled company, is "read out," and his stripes are ceremoniously ripped off. The result of the degradation is a change of status for the offender, and the significance of that change is that it constitutes a change in his eligibilities to participate in certain ways (as certain Elements) in the social life of the group. In the military case, the degradation is literally a lowering of his grade or rank. The limiting case of degradation in this sense is total expulsion from the group via exile or death.

Garfinkel makes the following points about successful degradation ceremonies:

1. There must be a community of individuals who share certain

basic values such that adherence to those values is a condition for retaining good standing in the community, i.e., for being "one of us";

2. Three members of the community are involved, namely, a "Perpetrator," a "Denouncer," and (some number of) "Witnesses";

3. The Denouncer and the Witness act as members and representatives of the community and not out of merely personal interest;

4. The Denouncer describes the Perpetrator to the Witness as having committed a certain act;

5. The Denouncer redescribes the act (if necessary) in such a way that its incompatibility with the community's values follows logically;

6. The Denouncer presents a case for judging that the Perpetrator's engaging in the act (as redescribed) is a genuine expression of his character and is not to be excused or explained away by reference to accident, atypical states, etc.

Under these conditions, if the Denouncer makes his case successfully, he has thereby shown that the Perpetrator isn't now and *never really was* "one of us," and the degradation ceremony is successful.

In a BPU format this account could be represented as in Table 3a.

The elaboration of the first Stage in terms of Options could be accomplished as in Table 3b.

Note that in the absence of a specification of the Act, the Group, and their values, our decomposition quickly comes to an end, not from any formal necessity, but because we have no further information that requires it. From the standpoint of the degradation ceremony *as such*, we invoke LC-III because all that is required is that the processes we have represented in the BPU format should *occur*. Since LC-III gives an Event description, we can see why historical events should stand out as being what History is essentially

P-NameA: Degradation Ceremony
P-DescriptionA:
P-Paradigms: This is the only one.

(a) Stages:
>   (1) Description of the Act
>   (2) Redescription of the Act as reprehensible
>   (3) Characterization of the Perpetrator by the Act

Options:

See Table 3b.

(b) Individuals:

>   D, P, A, G, W_1, W_2, . . . , W_n

(c) Elements:
>   (1) Denouncer
>   (2) Perpetrator
>   (3) Act
>   (4) Witness
>   (5) Group

(d) Eligibilities:
>   D = Denouncer
>   P = Perpetrator
>   A = Act
>   G = Group
>   W = Witness

(e) Contingencies:
>   (1) D, P, W have been bona fide members of G
>   (2) D, W share basic values of G
>   (3) D and W represent G, not themselves
>   (4) Stage 2 only if stage 1
>   (5) Stage 3 only if stage 2

P-NameA1:   Description of the Act
P-DescriptionA1:   D gives W to understand that P committed A
   Option 1.   (D tells W)
     P-NameA11:   D tells W that P committed A
       Stage 1.   D says "P"
       Stage 2.   D says "committed"
       Stage 3.   D says "A"
     Individuals, Elements, etc., same as in Table 3a BPU
   Option 2.   (D writes to W)
     P-NameA12:   D writes to W that P committed A, etc.

or typically interested in (Gruner, 1969). It is not that those events have some recondite character which makes them peculiarly relevant to historical study (and similarly for behavioral events and behavioral science). Rather, it is that the historian's way (and the behavioral scientist's way) of taking an interest in what actually happens defines as a boundary condition the mere occurrence of what is of interest, and that is given by an Event description (LC-III and Rule 10a).

On the other hand, if the specifications of Act, Group, values, etc., were given, we might well be overwhelmed by the number of Versions it would be possible to distinguish. For example, what is the range of ways in which D could give W to understand that P committed A? Consider, for example, that Marc Antony's funeral oration was a denunciation; yet, it is quite certain that no behavioral scientist who was involved in charting Degradation Ceremony Versions would think of that one even as a possibility until he actually encountered it. Evidently, our descriptions will routinely employ a "wastebasket" category—"The Versions of P-NameA are $V_1, V_2, \ldots, V_n$, and W," where W = "any other way that P-NameA could happen." This will be the functional equivalent of formulating "precise" and "determinate" generalizations or theories in the pictorial tradition and, in that tradition, leaving the essential qualifications to be stated elsewhere and elsewhen in "methodological" terms—"But, of course, since these general descriptions have an 'open texture', don't be surprised if they don't quite fit the facts or if they are exemplified in surprising ways."

B. OBJECT DESCRIPTION

Since composition and decomposition of objects and processes involve a part-whole relationship in either case, we may use the analysis of process as a point of reference for generating systematic object descriptions. The directly relevant Transition Rules here are the following:

1. A state of affairs is a totality of related objects and/or processes and/or events and/or states of affairs.

2. Any process or object or event or state of affairs is a state of affairs which is a constituent of some other state of affairs.

3. An object is a state of affairs having other, related objects as constituents

8a. That a given object or process or event has a given relation to another object or process or event is a state of affairs.

9. That a given object, process, event, or state of affairs is of a given kind is a state of affairs.

As in the case of process analysis, the systematization of Object description is accomplished by setting up a recursive unit (the Basic Object Unit) in a "Name" and "Description" format and introducing ancillary resources for dealing with recursively generated representations and contextual features. The first of these, the Basic Object Unit, or BOU, is shown in Table 4a; the second is given in Table 4b.

As in the case of the Basic Process Unit, part of the BOU is designed to codify the compositional and decompositional aspect of Object representation and part is designed to reflect the state-of-affairs structure of a given object. The recursive structure is given

---

TABLE 4a   *Basic Object Unit (BOU)*

O-NameA: An expression which identifies the object. (This may be expanded to a list of names, each of which is the name of this same object.)

O-DescriptionA: The "description" of O-NameA. It specifies:
O-Paradigms 1, 2, . . . , n. These are alternative decompositions of O-NameA into immediate constituents. For each paradigm, specify:

(1) *Constituents*: A list of immediate constituents, which for systematic purposes may be designated as O-Name1A1, O-Name1A2, . . . , for paradigm 1; O-Name 2A1, O-Name 2A2, . . . , for paradigm 2, etc. (In practice, such "descriptive" names as "carburetor," "hand," "pancreas" will also be used.) Each such constituent can now be decomposed by being given a BOU representation.

(2) *Relationships* 1, 2, . . . , m: These are given by a list of relationships. Each item on the list is specified as follows.
(A) Name: An expression which identifies an N-place relationship (state of affairs). Note that n is not constant for different elements of the list 1, 2, . . . , m.
(B) Elements: A list of N Elements, each of which is one of the members of the N-place relationships.
(C) Individuals: A list of individuals which are constituents of O-Name1A.
(D) Eligibilities: A specification of which individuals may or must participate as which Elements in the relationship by virtue of their constituency in O-Name1A.
(E) Contingencies (Attributional or co-occurrence): Specification of conditions under which an individual eligible to be a given Element is that Element.

(3) *Attributes* of O-Paradigm (i.e., of O-NameA as consisting of the structure given by the relationship involved in a given paradigm).

For O-NameA, specify:
  (1) Attributes of O-NameA
  (2) Contingencies:
      (A) Attributes which a given constituent must have.
      (B) Applicability of a given name, e.g., O-Name2A3, as presupposing a given O-paradigm or a recursive elaboration of one.
      (C) Applicability of a given name as presupposing a unit (e.g., object, process, configuration) of which O-NameA is a constituent. (Most technical terminology would fall under this heading—recall "the physical world," "the baseball world," etc.)
      (D) Configuration (etc.) membership or attributes of O-NameA as contingent on the specification of a given O-Paradigm, KA, or
      (E) on given attributes of a given constituent (e.g., an automobile is an internal combustion machine because its motor is an internal combustion machine).
  (3) Relationships: As in 4a, above, but not restricted to immediate constituents as Elements.
  (4) (Optional convenience) Configuration membership: A list of configurations of which O-NameA may be a constituent.

by the Name, Description, O-Paradigm, and constituents aspects. The state-of-affairs structure is given by the Relationships and Contingencies. The Attribute and constituency aspects are redundant features designed to facilitate compositional representation.

Given the simple and extended BOU, more complex structures are generated by composition in terms of configuration (see (4) of the extended BOU) or by decomposition in terms of constituents (see (1) of the BOU). These recursively generated structures are held together primarily by the relationships implied by the immediate constituent breakdown (Rule 3) and by the immediate constituency relationship itself. In addition, Relationships (Table 4a(2) and Contingencies (Table 4b(2)C and 4b(3)) may connect constituents at any level of compositional and decompositional representation.

It is abundantly evident from the complex structure of the BOU that to say merely that one object is "part of" another object or that one object is "composed of" other objects is to give an extremely incomplete and noncommittal description of some state of affairs. For one object, B, cannot be part of another object, A, pure and simple without being some particular part, any more than it could just be colored without having any particular color. B must correspond to some derivation from some O-paradigm of A; and it is this derivation which determines *which* part of A, B is, what the other, correlative parts of B are, and what B's relationships to those other parts must or may be. Thus, O-NameA is not merely not the same thing as its parts and not merely not the same thing as the "sum" of its parts, it is not the same thing as its parts in any relationship except one which they may have by virtue of being the Elements they are in the state of affairs which *is* the same thing as O-NameA.

And "B," the referring term for the constituent, may be a name which presupposes that B is part of A (exemplifying Table 4b(2)C, e.g., "citizen," "professor," "lieutenant colonel," "meson," "experience," "stimulus"), in which case the statement that B is part of A is pre-empirical; or it may not, in which case the statement that B is part of A is empirical or nonsensical.

To be sure, it is just that incompleteness of "B is part of A" which gives the part-whole relationship the great degree of generality that it has (recall LC-I) and which enables us to formulate so many of the basic Transition Rules and their technical elaborations in terms of the concept of "constituent."

C. CONFIGURATION DESCRIPTION

A Configuration description is one which represents a state of affairs either (a) as being an object (by Rule 3) and having process constituents or (b) as being a process (by Rule 5) and having object constituents.

Almost any object or process which is of any scientific interest and is not an "ultimate" object or process will qualify as a configuration, so that comprehensive scientific explanation will routinely take the form of Configuration description. We have seen that behavioral processes will involve objects, since at a minimum they will involve the individuals who are behaving. Conversely, a piece of machinery (organic or otherwise) or an organization of behaving individuals will be an object in which some of the relationships for which its constituents are eligible will be process relationships. Thus, although object and process concepts are the necessary ingredients, our major conceptual and experimental interest will be in configurational states of affairs, since that is the form in which we will represent most of what actually happens.

The way in which objects may be constituents in a process is, clearly, as Individuals which are eligible to be particular Elements in that Process. The way in which a process may be a constituent of (a state of affairs which is the same thing as) an object is given by (2)D of the Basic Object Unit. In (2)D a specification is given of which Individuals *may* or must participate as which Elements in the Relationship by virtue of their constituency in O-Name1A. One reason for the leeway here is that an object may have parts which are literally interchangeable (e.g., the tires on an automobile) or functionally interchangeable (e.g., the top and bottom of a symmetric ashtray). The second reason is to allow for the occurrence of a process involving those parts which have optional relationships. The specification of a process involving some parts of an object (e.g., a running motor, a person walking or digesting food) will be the specification of a sequence of such optional relationships, and the non-necessity of the occurrence of the process will be codified

55

by a Contingency statement (4a(2)E) specifying the conditions under which it will occur. If no Description of the process can be given, then the process Name (e.g., "walks") may be used as an Attribute of the object (4a(3) or 4b(1)).

Some of the major characteristics of a configuration will reflect the object-process contrast. If the configuration is an object (with process constituents) it will have the general character of a "system," whereas, if it is a process (with object constituents) it generally will not. Thus, for example, a stable society or other social organization will be perspicuously represented as a self-maintaining system, whereas one which is progressively deteriorating, explosively expanding, or radically metamorphosing generally will not.

Perspicuous or not, one may always adopt one or the other form of representation and one may adopt a "theoretical" language that is committed to the chosen form of representation. That will frequently give the impression of having made a factual commitment about the nature of social organization and social change.

D. CHRONOLOGICAL DESCRIPTION

Each of the forms of description discussed above (and below) is "repeatable" in the sense that it would be possible to encounter more than one phenomenon which would satisfy a particular description having that form. In contrast, the Chronology is a form of description which corresponds to Limiting Case I, i.e., the real world. As such, it is necessarily nonrepeatable.

If A and A′ are distinct phenomena identified by the applicability of the single description "Q," e.g., "degradation ceremony," "eclipse," "mitosis," then each of A and A′ is a state of affairs. In that case, there is another state of affairs, C, having A and A′ as constituents (Rule 1, 2, 8). Moreover, A and A′ have some set of relationships, R_1, R_2, . . . , R_K, such that their having those relationships is the state of affairs K (Rule 8); then, either K is a constituent of C or K is identical to C. Thus, repetition of what satisfies a given State-of-Affairs description is necessarily relative to some wider state-of-affairs context within which the repetition occurs. A phenomenon for which no wider context exists is necessarily nonrepeatable, and that condition is satisfied uniquely by LC-I, namely, the state of affairs of which all other states of affairs are constituents.

Chronology is therefore a description of historical particulars. The general form of a Chronology is that of a Configuration description. What distinguishes it from Configuration description per se is its nonrepeatability by virtue of its unlimited scope.

We do not, of course, have descriptions of the whole world. Rather, we give Chronological descriptions of some parts and aspects of the real world by using more or less incomplete Configuration descriptions. In giving such descriptions, we are committed to their (the configurations being described) being parts of the history of the world. That is to say that we are committed to there being a "world formula," corresponding to the real world, part of which is identical to the Configuration description we have given. Since that part is a particular part of a nonrepeatable whole, it is itself nonrepeatable.

One sort of description which necessarily carries this commitment is an observation report (this is an instance of Contingency (2)C in the extended BOU). The uniqueness of the real world is a consequence of its nonrepeatability; but any of the finite states of affairs which can be represented by a State-of-affairs description is, *as such*, repeatable in the sense given above. What gives historical states of affairs their historical uniqueness is their relationship to an object whose historical uniqueness is guaranteed, namely, an observer. For any observer, the real world is necessarily the world which includes him as an observer.

It is commonly supposed that historical uniqueness is secured by assigning space-time coordinates or the functional equivalent thereof to the phenomenon in question. But one can do this for a fictional account of a fictional world no less than for a factual account of the real world. My reference to the overthrow of the Cthulu in the year 653 is a fictional reference because I don't take myself to have any position on that calendar or on that geography. In contrast, my reference to the discovery of America in 1492 is a factual reference because I do take myself to have a position (1973) on the same calendar and on the same geography. Moreover, that calendar and that geography have a place for the *fictional* reference to the overthrow of the Cthulu.

Thus, "what actually happens" is Chronology. What actually happens is historically unique and that uniqueness depends on the historical uniqueness of observers and their observational and descriptive achievements. (This is a conceptual necessity, not a phenomenological discovery.) *What* it is that actually happens is, for a given observer, given by what he observes to be the case, augmented by his explanatory or systematic elaborations thereof. The empiricist principle that our knowledge of the real world is ultimately empirical (grounded in observation) is intelligible in this way as a nonempirical principle.

E.   MEANS-ENDS DESCRIPTION

Means-Ends descriptions are incomplete Process descriptions, and the sense in which they are incomplete is best exhibited by reference to the notion of "Element" in the Basic Process Unit. We noted that one implicit contingency statement was "if the requisite Elements are not present the process will not take place." Means-Ends descriptions are specifications of a set of Elements which is sufficient for some Version of the process in question. The set of Elements would, in general, vary from Version to Version.

What is left out of the Means-Ends description is the process structure, the representation of how and in what order those Elements enter into the process, and what the alternative Versions are.

Since a Process representation may be a hierarchical, recursively generated structure of subprocesses, it would be possible to have a complex Process representation which contained Means-Ends descriptions instead of Process descriptions at the most detailed level of description.

Frequently, Means-Ends descriptions are given in place of behavioral process descriptions when the knowledge and competence of the user of the description can be counted on to fill in or compensate for the descriptive deficit. Very often this contribution by the user is essential, since the describer will not be able to give a full Process description (in some cases, because there isn't that kind of regularity or patterning involved).

F.   TASK DESCRIPTION OR ACHIEVEMENT ANALYSIS

If a Means-Ends analysis is a statement of what is sufficient for the accomplish*ing* of a given result, a Task analysis is a statement of what is sufficient to qualify as the accomplish*ment* of a given result. The paradigmatic locutions for a task analysis are (1) "To accomplish P, R, and S *is* to accomplish Q" and (2) "To accomplish P, R, and S is *a* way to accomplish Q." Formally, the procedure is to begin with a State-of-Affairs description, "Q," and associate with it a set of more limited states of affairs which jointly exemplify Q or are equivalent to Q.

For an example of a Task analysis, we need look no further than the original account of degradation ceremonies which was used to exemplify a Process representation. The title of the original, "Conditions of Successful Degradation Ceremonies," is ambiguous and could equally well be taken to refer to a Means-Ends analysis, a

Task analysis, or a set of contingency statements in a Process description. Indeed, there might be some question, even upon reading the entire article, as to whether Garfinkel was offering an empirical generalization (of causal conditions or procedural rules of thumb) or a conceptual analysis. However, if we ask how much and what part of a Process representation of degradation ceremonies is provided, it appears clearly that what we are given is a Task analysis along the lines of locution (1), i.e., "To accomplish P, R, and S *is* to accomplish Q." Thus it is a conceptual analysis, not an empirical generalization.

As we look back at the Process representation given above for the degradation ceremony, we can see that, although the order there is intuitively reasonable, in fact no order is prescribed. The stages *could* be interchanged. For example, D might make the case that if P *were* to engage in A that *would* be an expression of his character, then typify the act as contrary to Group values, and conclude with a dramatic "And he did do A!" Or again, all three might be accomplished more or less simultaneously. For example, in the military situation, the single reading "Carlyle, you vile, treacherous coward who left your comrades to die, you're a disgrace to the Queen's uniform," accompanied by the ripping off of Carlyle's stripes, might do the job. In a Process representation, these possibilities would most likely be represented as different Versions and perhaps would be derived from different Paradigms.

The relationships among Task analyses, Means-Ends descriptions, and Process representations are conducive to certain systematic ambiguities. For example, in a behavioral context a Task analysis will automatically qualify as a Means-Ends description in the ordinary manner of speaking. For, if to accomplish P, R, and S is to accomplish Q or is a way of accomplishing Q, then accomplishing P, R, and S is a means to accomplishing Q, and it is a procedure for accomplishing Q. Also, if "accomplishing P" is taken as the name of a process which results in P, it may also be taken as the name of an event, namely, the accomplishment of P, and as the name of a different event, namely, the occurrence of the process which resulted in P. It is by virtue of this ambiguity that one can say simply that historical events are the subject matter of History, that behavioral events are the subject matter of behavioral science, etc.

The same relationships which generate the ambiguities are also a positive representational resource. Among other things, Task analysis appears to be indispensable in representing certain kinds of social practices which are "free," "flexible," or "open-ended" in certain respects. Consider, for example, a type of meeting which we may call a "Leader-Agenda Group." This is a task-oriented group, presided over by a leader, which takes up one topic (task) after another. An examination of a transcript of such a meeting showed no obvious sequential structure or contingencies, and it was clear that there was no way of specifying for the general case any particular number, order, or set of topics discussed. Very little sequential structure was obvious within any given topic discussion, either.

The practice was analyzed by reference to a repeating unit consisting of dealing with a single agenda item, or Topic. A Task analysis of the Topic was made in terms of four lists of elements, namely, (1) general context of the topic "why are we doing this?" (2) decisions to be made or alternatives to be selected among, (3) generally relevant considerations, and (4) those considerations favoring one choice over another. The Elements for the process consisted of L (the leader) and M_1, M_2, . . . , M_K (members). Constituent subprocesses (recursive) consisted of Presentation-Response units where the Presentation consisted initially of introducing an item on one of the four lists and the Response involved the Options of (1) doing nothing, (2) adding to the Presentation, (3) elaborating on the Presentation, (4) challenging, and (5) questioning. The recursive structure here consisted in the Contingency that any Response could be treated as a Presentation, thereby generating a new Response, etc. (Had the presentations of items on the four lists been represented as Elements, e.g., Act 1, . . . , N, then the same result would be given by saying that any Individual that was a Response Act was eligible to be a Presentation Act also.)

A discursive rendering of the Process analysis (of the Leader-Agenda Group meeting) which employed the Task analysis as an essential component would go roughly as follows: The Leader was eligible to introduce Topics and make Presentations which were not Responses. Members were eligible to make Responses to Presentations, and everyone was eligible to treat a Response as a Presentation and respond to it (i.e., every item on one of the lists could itself become a miniature Topic, and the sequential structure was of a "last in, first out" variety). Everyone was eligible to make a special Presentation Option initiating a decision (i.e., call for a vote). Members were eligible to present Topics after the Leader's agenda was completed.

In this way it was possible to do substantial descriptive justice both to the lack of antecedently specifiable content, sequence, or number of stages and to the kind of structure which makes the operation of such a group the familiar and usually orderly process it is. In general, it appears that a certain kind of open-endedness is defined by an optional recursiveness contingent on the behavioral Option selection by Elements.

G. Event Description

The descriptive format for representing events is formally one of the simplest of those considered here. The primarily relevant Transition Rules are the following:

6. An event is a direct change from one state of affairs to another.

7. An event is a state of affairs having two states of affairs (i.e., "before" and "after") as constituents.

10. That an object or process begins is an event and that it ends is a different event.

If we keep to the "Name" and "Description" format, then Rule 7 directly provides the form of the "Description." That is, we specify the two states of affairs, SA1 and SA2, and this, together with a Name which identifies the event (SA3), will provide the representation of that event.

The simplicity is only a formal one, however, for there are de facto ambiguities and complexities to be dealt with.

One such consideration is that most frequently our discursive references to events involves a confounding of "Name" and an incomplete "Description," namely, SA2. "The light bulb exploded," "He won the race," "It occurred to him that . . ." are examples of specifying SA2, i.e., what the change was a change *to*.

A second consideration is that the event, and the representation of it, may indeed be extremely complex. All that is required is that either SA1 or SA2 be complex states of affairs, and then the change from one to another will be complex. One common kind of complexity stems from the fact that SA1 or SA2 may have to be specified by Configuration descriptions, for example, "The automobile backfired," or "The battle took place," or "The anemia improved."

Or again, the specification of an event may be accomplished discursively by giving a categorization of SA3 (SA3 includes SA1 and SA2), i.e., by saying not what changed into what, but rather what kind of change it was. "The anemia *improved*" is an example here. In this case it is Rule 9 that is involved. And in this case it is frequently possible to reconstruct a relation between SA1 and SA2. For example, "The anemia improved" suggests strongly that SA2 involves a greater number of red blood cells than does SA1. And finally, such reconstruction is possible normally by virtue of such contingencies as 4b(2)C, D, and E in the BOU. That is, terms such as "red blood cell" are O-Names which identify an object *as* a particular constituent of a particular other kind of object (here, a certain class of organisms) and as derived from the latter via a particular O-Paradigm. (The O-Paradigm required by "red blood cell" was, for example, unknown to the Greeks and Romans, although some of the O-Names, e.g., "human bodies," were quite well known then.)

Still, the formal simplicity of Event description is a genuine one. The complexities here arise from the convertibility of Event representations to Object, Process, and State-of-Affairs representations. Event representation shares the possible complexities of these latter but adds little of its own.

H. STATE-OF-AFFAIRS DESCRIPTION

State-of-Affairs description is of particular interest for two reasons. First, if any of the reality concepts could be said to have priority over the others, it is the concept of "state of affairs." Object, Process, and Event descriptions may be converted into one another, but only by being converted into SA descriptions first. Moreover, it is only those Transition Rules which concern states of affairs which also involve relations and properties (being of a certain kind—Rule 9). Finally, as we shall see later, other kinds of concepts are essential only insofar as they are required to distinguish one state-of-affairs concept from another. It is from these various considerations that the reality system given by the Transition Rules was designated as the SA system.

The second reason for the particular interest is that State-of-Affairs description is what is accomplished directly in the asserting

64

or statement-making use of either ordinary language or technical language. Observation reports, theoretical statements, "lawlike" generalizations, and explanations of any scientific kind will all have the status of State-of-Affairs descriptions. To relate this notion to some historical distinctions, the concept of a state of affairs is, for many purposes, the same thing as the classical "proposition," and descriptive language is essentially propositional and distinguished by its eligibility for truth and falsehood.

On the other hand, a proposition is not exclusively or primarily associated with a description and truth-eligibility, since it can also figure in a question, a supposition, a conjecture, a wish, a command, etc. As I indicated earlier, the declarative sentences in the present paper should not be understood as statements, but rather as instructions or exhortations modeled on the lines of "Notice this, i.e. [sentence], aspect of the conceptual structure I am *presenting herewith.*" It is because language is indispensable in giving us access to the state-of-affairs concepts which are indispensable in our behavior (and that is their only reality status), including our descriptive scientific behavior, that the articulation of "reality" requires for its completion the concept of language in addition to the concepts of person and behavior.

The most directly relevant Transition Rules for State-of-Affairs description are as follows:

1. A state of affairs is a totality of related objects and/or processes and/or events and/or states of affairs.

9. That a given object, process, event, or state of affairs, is of a given kind is a state of affairs.

8. That a given state of affairs has a given relation (e.g., succession, incompatibility, difference, inclusion, common constituency) to a second state of affairs is a state of affairs.

3. An object is a state of affairs having other, related objects as immediate constituents.

5. A process is a state of affairs having other, related processes as immediate constituents.

6. An event is a direct change from one state of affairs to another.

With regard to an explicit representational format for State-of-Affairs description, we may keep the standard "Name" and "Description" form and use the precedents provided by the BPU and BOU. Table 5 shows the State-of-Affairs Unit (SAU), which is modeled primarily on Rule 1. As in the other cases, the simple SAU is a recursive unit, and the full SAU shown in Table 5 involves one recursion in order that certain Contingencies may be simply stated.

TABLE 5 *State-of-Affairs Unit (SAU)*

SA-NameA: The "Name" of state of affairs A. This may be given by any identifying reference, such as a sentence ("The man shot the bear"), a sentential clause ("the shooting of the bear"), a simpler locution ("the shooting"), or a conventional symbol (SA-NameA).

SA-DescriptionA: The "Description" of SA-NameA. It specifies:

(I) *Relationship*: An explicit identification of an N-place relationship, or attribute. (A property is a 1-place attribute.)

(II) *Elements*: A list of the N elements, or logical roles in the Relationship. These are distinguished as 1st, 2nd, . . . , Nth elements.

(IIa) *Eligibilities*: Each of the N elements is characterized as being either necessarily or optionally an object, process, event, state of affairs, attribute, or concept.

(III) *Individuals*: A list of N Individuals identified *as* individuals by a name, number, symbol, etc. (Note that "individual" is *not* the same as "object.")

(IIIa) *Classification*: Each of the N individuals is identified as an object, process, event, state of affairs, attribute, or concept.

66

(IV) *Assignments*: The N Individuals are placed in one-to-one relation with the N Elements, with each Individual being identified as *the* exemplar of the corresponding Element in *the* state of affairs SA-NameA.

(V) *Expansions*: An expansion consists of the recursive use of the SAU (as developed to this point) in one of the following ways:

(1) Elaborating the Classification of a given Individual as an object, process, event, or state of affairs by giving a SAU description of it (via Rule 1, 3, 5, or 6). This will amount to using BPU, BOU, Event, or SAU formats.

(2) Elaborating the Classification of a given Individual as an Attribute by giving a SAU description in which the Attribute is the Relationship.

(VI) *Contingencies*:

(1) Since contingency statements are possible within BPU and BOU representations and the latter may occur as expansions, such contingency statements will qualify as contingencies within the full SAU also.

(2) Co-occurrence constraints such that the use of a particular "Name" (in general, referring terminology, either technical or nontechnical) for any Element within the full SAU is contingent on the use of particular other "Names" for other Elements.

(3) Co-occurrence constraints such that the use of a particular Element is contingent on its being that element (or an Element) of the SAU within which it is an Element. (Note that stages, options, and paradigms within a BPU or BOU will qualify as Elements here.)

Because of the equivalence of State-of-Affairs representation with the descriptive use of natural language, including technical or theoretical language, a major portion of the discussion of the significance of SA representation must wait on the systematic development of the concept of language in a subsequent paper. In the present context, certain comments are to the point.

(A) First, we may note from the Transition Rules that among the six basic reality concepts, it is only the concept of "state of affairs" which directly connects with all the other concepts simultaneously, and it is by virtue of this that the others are connected to one another. Because of this formal ubiquity, there is no part or aspect of any possible world to which State-of-Affairs representation would not provide *direct* descriptive access. However, since composition and decomposition of objects and processes cannot both be exhausted in principle (only by *fiat*, for a given individual), State-of-Affairs representation cannot provide *exhaustive* descriptive access to any part of any real world. Nor can any other form of representation.

Certain contrasts and similarities are of some interest here. For example, a pictorial representation provides direct access to some objects, processes, events, and states of affairs, but it is incomplete even with respect to these. Normal discursive description, whether technical or vernacular and whether observational or explanatory, is also both direct and incomplete. It is because of this similarity that traditional scientific theories, though discursive, exhibit the "pictorial perspective" referred to in Section II. In contrast, the SA system, as a calculational system, provides exhaustive access in principle, but it is *indirect*. The SA system is not itself a form of representation, but rather a codification of the capability of generating such forms. However, it is not exhaustive in practice, since we cannot in fact give a final and definitive specification of all the *kinds* of objects, processes, events, relations, and concepts which *could* be used in representing the real world.

(B) Second, the incompleteness of discursive representations of states of affairs is both an indispensable analytic resource and a source of considerable ambiguity and misunderstanding.

To see in what way it is analytically indispensable, let us first imagine a tremendously complex portion of the real world, such that a SAU representation would involve a network of objects, processes, events, and states of affairs, all decomposed recursively through some number of repetitions, and with contingencies crossing the lines of recursion. Such a configuration, or state of affairs, would be extraordinarily difficult to represent. If we were doing that, we should want to do it bit by bit, since it could hardly be done in one grand stroke. Moreover, ordinarily, we are not engaged in such representation. Rather, we are interested in some part, aspect, or feature of a configuration. If we had to generate a complex representation whenever we had anything to say, discourse as we know it would be impossible. Thus, State-of-Affairs description is indispensable because it is this form of description which enables us to connect any element (object, process, etc.) to any one or more others directly and without reference to the remainder of the complex. It is in this way that State-of-Affairs representation gives us direct access to any part and any aspect of a real world. (Compare Wittgenstein: "The world is everything that is the case. The world divides into facts, not things.")

Thus, the state-of-affairs system has, in this sense, an unlimited plasticity as a representational system (I have sometimes suggested that it can be understood as the real world analogue of the notion of "coordinate system" in the worlds of mathematics and physics). That is, it has an unlimited capacity for absorbing or codifying observational "facts" and unlimited richness for supplementing observation with explanatory accounts of "what actually happens" by reference to hypothetical objects, processes, events, states of affairs, and relationships. Doubtless, this is what has rendered the system as such invisible to the naked eye, as it were, and tempted our theologically disposed "tough-minded empiricists" (Smart, Skinner, et al.) to suppose that there is purely and simply a "natural order" of things "out there" as though the possibility of such things were not also a distinctively human invention. (Recall the strain between the methodological and historical connections between science, or logic, and the real world.)

However, it is partly because a discursive State-of-Affairs description may connect any set of elements within a much more extensive and complex SA structure that most such descriptions carry a heavy burden of presupposition or ambiguity. In referring to a part or aspect of some configuration it may be important to keep in the picture the fact that it is such a part or aspect. This can be managed effectively by adopting a distinctive terminology for dealing with any aspect or part of that configuration. This sort of bookkeeping is accomplished by Contingencies such as (2)B, (2)C, and (2)D in the BOU and VI(2) and VI(3) in the SAU. I have earlier referred to such devices as "Partial Description" (*Persons*, 1966a). Since a configuration is a domain of facts, the foregoing has direct application to the various sciences, disciplines, and fields of knowledge as well as distinctive human endeavors. The jargon associated with biology, economics, baseball, et cetera, will have as one of its primary functions the identification of the field of endeavor in which the jargon has its paradigmatic use.

The second reason for the ambiguity is that discursive State-of-Affairs representation is in effect (and almost literally so) a concatenation of "Names" as contrasted with "Descriptions" of the elements it brings together in a single state of affairs. This is a particularly outstanding feature of explanatory scientific accounts of unobservable entities. To put the ambiguity of discursive description in these terms is to show the advantage of the requirement, for scientific practice, of an alternative, *systematic* representation of what is observedly, reportedly, and purportedly "what actually happens." In the final section, this advantage will be illustrated in connection with certain problems concerning scientific explanation and description.

IV

"WHAT ACTUALLY HAPPENS" IN SOME SCIENCE-RELATED AREAS

IN THE PRECEDING SECTION forms of representation of what "happens" or "is the case" were presented. The representational formats are conceptually derived technical devices which provide the public, observable, manipulable correlatives of the corresponding reality concepts. As is the case with concepts, forms of representation are *ineligible* for truth values, assumptions, implications, belief, doubt, or evidence. The use of conceptual distinctions is presupposed by any of these latter. Thus, concepts and forms of representation are pre-empirical.

However, the employment of a new form of representation may, nevertheless, enable us to command a clearer view of those matters which we find both problematical and engaging. It may also enable us to find problematical or simply false or patently ridiculous certain "obvious truths." In either case, it may suggest new questions, new answers, and new things to do. I have indicated some of these innovations elsewhere (1969b).

The range of relevance of the Person Concept and the SA system portion of it extends beyond behavioral science or even science per se, and I think that in the interest of presenting these concepts there is a point in illustrating that kind of application without going too far afield from behavioral science. Thus, in the present section we will consider briefly a formulation in History and a problem in Semantics. These topics are taken from the recent literature and appear to reflect an upsurge of interest in reality concepts. Indeed, the fact of encountering a number of such discussions was one of the factors that prompted the present effort; for the original formulation of the SA system (1966b) was made at a time when there was little interest in "ontology," so that that formulation was subsequently presented only in relatively technical contexts (1969b, 1971), a minor example of the historical connection between science and the real world.

A.   HISTORICAL EXPLANATION AND SUBJECT MATTER

In an effort to explicate the nature of the phenomena which are the subject matter of historical explanations, Gruner (1969) provides a systematic look at the concepts of "object," "event," and "state of affairs." That the nature of historical explanation is, in turn, of potentially central importance for behavioral science is illustrated by the continuing repercussions of Dray's (1957) challenge to the causal model of explanation which has dominated the history of behavioral science. Because of Dray's influence, the central issue raised by reference to historical explanation is generally taken to be the issue of action-rationale (norm-governed, rule-following) explanations versus predictive regularity (lawlike, nomothetic) explanations. And it is hardly accidental that the question of reference is raised by Cohen (see below) in connection with the description of actions.

But one can think of additional reasons why it is History rather than, say, Economics or Political Science which has been the touchstone of controversy. Whether historians fully approve or not, it is a truism that History is the study of *what actually happened*. It is this notion which leads Gruner, as a historian, to make systematic reference to objects, events, and states of affairs.

A background for Gruner's reference to these reality concepts is provided by the fact that a central part of the cultural inheritance of both modern History and behavioral science is the notion of the physical world as the Given and as the wider stage within which behavioral-social phenomena take place. Thus, when referring expressions such as "event," "object," or "state of affairs" are used descriptively, e.g., in reporting an observation, it is commonly supposed that these terms function as does the pronoun "it" or the demonstrative "this," i.e., that they serve to pick out the thing that is referred to but in no way characterize it. The "thing" they pick out is, on this view, antecedently given as a *physical* object, event, etc. It is not surprising, therefore, that little attention has been paid to the possibility that "event," "object," etc., have logical relations to one another and to other concepts, since it is more or less taken for granted that, outside of mathematical and other formal systems, logical relations are a feature of the meaning of a term, and since purely referring expressions have no meaning they ought not to have any logical relations either. (See also the later discussion of "being informative.")

But Gruner points out that "As with many other words, the usefulness of 'event' depends on a contrast or comparison with other things, and only if there are historical phenomena which cannot rightly be called events has the term any significance." His analysis is that when an event occurs something changes, and that something is a state, condition, or state of affairs. (Recall Rule 6.) But states or conditions must be conditions *of* something, and so a state requires a thing or object as its subject: "An object R is in a state S_1; an event E happens; and R's state S_1 is replaced by another state, S_2." For Gruner, this single statement captures the basic interrelations among "object," "event," and "state." His further, informal elaboration includes the following:

1. Events do not change, hence cannot have duration. Since achievements (or more generally, results) cannot be conceived of as having duration, achievement words are the only words that always refer to events.

2. A battle, which is time-extended, may be thought of as changing a state, e.g., the political or military state of a country. Hence we may allow time-extended events by recognizing that *something is an event only relative to something else.*

3. If we allow time-extended events, it will be a matter of choice whether one wishes to speak of a single event or a number of events. A battle, for example, consists of many separate episodes (subevents), each of which possesses its own subevents. (Recall Rule 5.)

4. The relation between an extended event and its subevents is neither causal nor analytic.

5. What is from one point of view an event may, from another point of view, be an object and, from still another, a state. For example, a battle can be thought of as an object whose states are being changed. And, for example, if the battle "becomes a scramble for plunder," then it is a kind of state.

6. This relativity can be extended to historical ideas, not to mention social and other institutions. ("The idea of 'progress' is not in the same healthy state today as it was in the nineteenth century.")

7. To locate the event character in the eye of the describer is not to deny reality in any meaningful sense of this word to any individual historical phenomena. ("There still was, or occurred, a French Revolution, whether the item that goes by this name is conceived as an event, or as a state, or as an object.")

8. But there are limits. In History, at least, it is impossible to

conceive of physical objects, including [*sic*] human individuals, as anything but objects, as things which are in states.

9. "One may conceive of an historical process as a continuous and even flow, but when it is a matter of putting things down on paper and of writing history, one cannot do without events."

To these considerations, Walsh (1969) adds:

8a. Once it is granted that nations, institutions, and perhaps even processes could all be regarded as objects, there should be no difficulty in thinking of a person, such as Napoleon, as an event. "We do that, indeed, when we speak of him as a 'phenomenon.'" (Recall Rules 10, 10a.)

10. Although nations are not separately identified entities over and above their members, it is nations and institutions and other social groupings which are more centrally the subject of History than individual persons.

In summary, Gruner succeeds in making a case for logical relations among "event," "state," and "object" such that these apply *as descriptions* only relative to one another. He indicates further that contextual possibilities are always such that what is describable in any of these ways is describable in each of these ways, with a corresponding change in the reference of the other two associated terms. An exception to this interchangeability (but not the relativity) is made with respect to those objects which he regards as the fundamental subject matter of History, i.e., persons (the "ultimate object" for historical facts) and "other [*sic*] physical objects." Walsh notes that this exception is formally arbitrary, questions the notion that individual persons are the central subject matter of History, and raises the issue of reductionism in thinking of nations and institutions as "mere 'logical constructions' out of individual persons."

It seems clear that both in general tenor and specific detail Gruner's discussion represents a partial formulation of the SA system presented above in Table 1. The substantial deficits in Gruner's formulation leave little doubt that the rationale for historical subject matter and explanation cannot be given by the partial formulation. For example:

1. It is one thing to remind us of logical connections among the three concepts and another to make these connections coherent and intelligible. The formulation of the SA system as a calculational system accomplishes the latter.

2. The equivocation or ambiguity of "event" as being either extended or not extended is certainly undesirable. This is too basic a difference, *pace* Ryle, to be left unsystematized. The missing ingredient here is obviously the concept of "process," which both Gruner and Walsh mention but do not exploit. A plausible reason for their failure to do so is contained in Gruner's reference to process as a "continuous flow." Such a process is indeed not what the historian needs, and so the common notion that a process is really a continuous process would rule out "process" as a basic concept for historians. In the SA formulation the concept of a discrete process is fundamental even though the Transition Rules also encompass continuous processes.

3. The relativity and interchangeability of "event," "object," and "state" appear to threaten a thoroughgoing fragmentation of the subject matter, hence also its explanatory reconstruction, since there does not seem to be any way of relating descriptions which overlap in their reference but are given from different viewpoints (e.g., the battle as a state versus the battle as an object versus the battle as a single event versus the battle as an extended event).

An important special case of this difficulty is this. If a nation can sensibly be conceived as an object and each of its citizens can be conceived as an object, surely we would require, at least as an option, that it be possible to speak of both nation and citizens as objects simultaneously. (Note that the logic here is the same as between an automobile and its carburetor or between a person and his liver.) Gruner's relativity formulation appears to rule out such an option. One consequence is the disagreement with Walsh as to which of these two kinds of object is *the* basic subject matter of History. Either way, the answer would be subject to Cohen's critique (below) of "*the* description" (of the basic object of historical study).

The SA system offers no such problems. The issue was discussed in Section III as the issue of enrichment versus replacement of descriptions. Gruner's relativity formulation appears to require replacement whereas Identity Coordination in the SA system permits both. And it is enrichment which permits the building up of "world formulas" which integrate, rather than fragment, a subject matter. For nations and citizens, Rule 3 is directly applicable.

4. "There still was, or occurred, a French Revolution, whether the item that goes by this name is conceived as an event, or as a state, or as an object." This formulation is directly vulnerable to Cohen's critique, below, i.e., "Just *what* 'item' is that?" A system with Identity Coordination does not encounter the pragmatic paradoxes associated with traditional theories of reference.

5. The (informal) definition of History in terms of either "basic object" of study (i.e., persons or nations and institutions) does not distinguish History from other behavioral sciences and disciplines. In this regard, the extended systematization of the reality concepts appears to provide the needed resource in the form of the "Chronological description." Traditionally, a contrast has been drawn between a historical account and a "mere chronology." (The latter is not to be confused with Chronological description.) A chronology is simply a sequential account, in observable, concrete

detail, of what happens. A history, in contrast, is an abstract account which reflects the historian's selection of significant detail.

Then does the historian not, after all, deal with what actually happens, and if he does is it only because History is merely "applied sociology"? The very compellingness of the history-chronology contrast appears to have left the historians with fundamental uncertainty in regard to whether there is any distinct subject matter for History and whether there is any distinctive "historical method" and whether History is distinct from social psychology or sociology and whether there is any "objective" way of distinguishing historically significant detail from mere chronological detail.

The SA system does not provide answers to such questions, but it does suggest that there is a point in talking about these matters in certain ways. To begin with, the SA formulation reminds us that the difference between History and chronology is not the difference between atomic facts and generalizations or "abstractions" therefrom. Since there is no description which *could* not be considered incomplete in regard to detail, a chronology, in the traditional definition, is not per se the distinctively historical formulation from which systematic historical accounts derive their distinctively historical character (in this sense, any empirical data is given first by a chronology). The distinctive character of History, therefore, is not to be sought for in data but rather in the type of explanatory formula which provides the paradigm cases of historical accounts (what constitutes "the historical world"). Such a formula may be found in the Chronological description of Section III. There we saw that what distinguishes Chronological description from, e.g., State-of-Affairs description or Configuration description is *not* either a distinctive set of happenings or a distinctive *form* of representation in any usual sense (historical descriptions would in general take the form of Configuration or SA descriptions), but rather the representation of a phenomenon *as* a portion of a nonrepeatable "world formula" which makes historical particulars both unique and uniquely cases of "what actually happens." Thus, both the distinctness from the other behavioral sciences and disciplines and the close relationship to at least some number of them is accounted for. History is no more "applied sociology" or "applied economics" than Astronomy or Cosmology are "applied physics."

B. THE PROBLEM OF REFERENCE AND DESCRIPTIONS OF "THE SAME THING"

As part of the background for Gruner's discussion of objects, events, and states, I indicated that the behavioral sciences and disciplines have inherited a heavy burden of philosophical theorizing about what there is and how we talk about it. Among the major burdens of this sort is the semantic "theory of reference" and a variety of "logical" or "methodological" formulations which incorporate such thinking. Historically, the notion that there is *a* something, a "referent," which any of our descriptions is merely in fact *about* has evolved as the notion that the something is physical and that physical objects, processes, etc., are what behavioral science descriptions, whether observational or explanatory, are in fact necessarily about. We find just such a notion expressed more or less explicitly by both Gruner and Walsh in their discussions of historical phenomena. It is hardly surprising, therefore, that the behavioral sciences have systematically excluded fundamental behavioral concepts and remained parasitical on the methodologically incomplete "natural" sciences. (See the discussion of "naturalism" in Section VI.) The notion that psychological, sociological, and other behavioral descriptions are just different ways of talking about the same, i.e., really physical, things has provided the major lines along which this parasitical dependency has been acted out, i.e.,

79

the "hypothesis" of "the unity of the sciences," at least in its vulgar form. The theory of reference itself, however, is being subjected to increasingly pointed criticism.

Cohen (1970) examines "the assumption by some recent philosophers that we can attach a clear sense to the claim that one and the same action can be described in many different ways." Consider the following sets of descriptions.

(a) Brutus killed Caesar with a knife.
(b) Brutus killed Caesar.
(c) Brutus killed Caesar in the Forum with a knife.
(d) He shot the bear with a revolver.
(e) He pointed the gun at the bear and pulled the trigger.
(f) The sheriff arranged for the official execution of a man he knew to be innocent.
(g) The sheriff arranged for the official execution of a man he knew to be innocent in order to save the lives of five other innocent men.
(h) The sheriff committed judicial murder.

Normally, we would say that if (a) Brutus killed Caesar with a knife, it follows straightforwardly that (b) Brutus killed Caesar. Yet there is no way in current logical theory to show this result. (In a similar case, Gruner points out that the relation between an extended event and a subevent is neither causal nor analytic; likewise, the occurrence of P-NameA (e.g., Dining) neither causes nor implies the occurrence of particular Versions or options (e.g., preparing steak). Cohen points out that Davidson's (1967) technique of "quantifying over events" as a way of getting at *the* event which, e.g. (a), (b), and (c) are all descriptions of will indeed work for examples such as (a) and (b), but when applied to cases such as (d) and (e) it leads to such absurdities as "He pulled the trigger with a revolver."

That the question of *the* description of the behavior (what the behavior really was) is not merely an academic matter is illustrated by cases such as (f), (g), and (h). In connection with such cases, Cody (1967) points out that

> Under one description a man is guilty of a crime or a sin. That, however, is just one of the many true descriptions of his action. Under still another, no legal or moral questions can be raised. Can there be justice in our praise or blame when everything depends on which description we select to judge a man's action under? It seems there cannot if many different descriptions are applicable and if all applicable descriptions are, though different, true.

Thus, there are two main questions here. The first is, What is it for there to be different descriptions of the same action (or the same anything)? Here, Cohen suggests that there is no answer, because ". . . that makes no sense unless you have a way of showing what action it is that they are both descriptions of; and I reject the view that some bodily movement is what provides the identity." He has also rejected other proposed ways of making the identification independently of any description.

The second question is, Given that there are several descriptions of the same action, which is *the* description? Cohen's answer here is, of course, negative. It also appears to be closely related to Gruner's "point of view" formulation: ". . . we might say that either description might count as the description of his action—provided we understand that this is not like saying 'the same action can be described in either way' as if it were a matter of a borderline case. It is just to say: You can regard *this* as the action, in which case the other is a description of its consequences; or you can regard the other as the action, in which case this is a description of how he did it." (See Ossorio, 1969b, 1973, for a systematic formulation of forms of behavior description.)

Cohen's critique appears to be well taken. Certainly, the standard theory of reference has been presented as though we could and do first pick out a bare particular and then sometimes go on to describe it. He rightly objects that in that case, unless we have a way of showing what actions two descriptions are descriptions of, it is ridiculous to go through the ceremony of saying that they are descriptions of the same action. (Compare: "I'm thinking a thought. Now I'm thinking the same thought again. Of course, I have no idea *what* thought it is.")

But, although Cohen shows what is unsatisfactory about simply saying, in the customary way, that (b) "Brutus killed Caesar" describes the same action as (a) "Brutus killed Caesar with a knife," it is equally unsatisfactory to have to conclude that it is nonsense to suppose that they do describe the same action. In the behavioral sciences we appear to have accepted both unsatisfactory consequences simultaneously. Because everybody knows that "every description is theory-laden" we regard all "data" with suspicion so long as they retain any distinctively behavioral flavor and are not merely a matter of assigning numbers to something or other. Correspondingly, behavioral concepts such as "behavior," "motivation," "learning," "personality," "cognition," and so on become expressions which can be defined only within a given theory. (See, e.g., Hall and Lindzey, 1971, p. 9). And intellectual anarchy is the predictable result, for there is no longer anything which might be called "personality" (etc.) which could serve as "the same thing" which various personality (etc.) theories provide different descriptions of. (See below on "Being Informative.") In effect, we accept Cohen's critique.

On the other hand, there is an equally general acceptance of an equally obvious truth, namely, that there is indeed a real description of what it is that behavioral theories are theories about; but it lies outside of behavioral science, in Biology, and ultimately in Physics; for everybody knows that persons are really organisms, and organisms are really et ceteras. If that real description is theory-laden, too, somehow it does not seem to matter there, perhaps because, after all, that is real science. In effect, we have never heard of Cohen's critique.

The SA-system formulation, involving the less-simplistic referential characteristic of Identity Coordination, does not create the problem of achieving a purely referential identification and thus offers a way to avoid the second of these embarrassing postures both in regard to actions and in regard to behavioral science. It also offers a way out of the first embarrassment because it provides a clear sense for the notion of there being different descriptions of the same thing.

With respect to actions, the indicated resolution hinges on (1) the part-whole relationships codified by the Transition Rules, (2) the notion of an incomplete description, and (3) the forms of representation which exhibit part-whole relationships and the constructive procedures of "composition" and "decomposition."

Cohen rightly rejects an informal, linguistic version of this resolution: "One might try to get around this by saying that 'Brutus killed Caesar' is really an ellipsis for 'Brutus killed Caesar with something.' But as Kenny has pointed out, it just isn't clear how long the unelliptical form of the sentence is; once one puts a restriction on the number of places available, one puts a restriction on the number of details which might be added to a description of Brutus' killing of Caesar, and it seems unlikely here that there be such a limit."

Note that this objection involves two points which were developed explicitly in Sections II and III. The first is the contrast between a description and a descriptive formula. The second is the reality constraint that no explicit representation of any part of a real world is also an exhaustive representation, since it always leaves room for further composition or decomposition. The solution which

Cohen rejects would involve a descriptive formula which (a) was only partially filled in with descriptive constants, hence was an incomplete description, and (b) was, except for the missing constants, an exhaustive representation of the behavioral episode in question. But we have seen that a descriptive formula cannot fulfill condition (b), and so this is not a possible solution.

However, such a formula is not needed, and a merely linguistic formulation will not be adequate. Let us first distinguish several states of affairs, SA1-SA6, and some corresponding descriptions, D1–D4, and some corresponding configurations, C1–C5. (All but one of the states of affairs will each be the same thing as a configuration. The descriptions will serve as the Names of the corresponding states of affairs or configurations.)

SA1 C1 D1 = "Brutus killed Caesar"

SA2 C2 D2 = "Brutus killed Caesar with a knife"

SA3 C3 D3 = "Brutus killed Caesar in the Forum with a knife"

SA4 C4 D4 = "what Brutus did to Caesar in the Forum"

SA5 C5 = any configuration which includes C1 and C2 as constituents

SA6 = any state of affairs which includes both SA1 and SA2 as constituents

Note that the required identification (What action is it that D1 and D2 are descriptions of?) will be provided by any description which is the Name of a state of affairs which qualifies as SA5 or SA6. For example, it will be provided by D3, since SA3 will qualify as SA6, and it will be provided by D4, since C4 qualifies as C5, hence SA4 qualifies as SA5. The details bear some discussion.

There are two possibilities here because there are two ways in which one might speak of "inclusion" here. SA5 is a case of one configuration including another configuration, as when the operation of a gasoline engine includes the operation of the carburetor. SA6 is a case of one fact including another fact, as when the fact that the object is a black, metal filing cabinet includes the fact that the object is black. We will examine these in order.

To be sure, one cannot move deductively from D4 "what Brutus did to Caesar in the Forum" to D1 "Brutus killed Caesar." Thus, it does not follow from D4 alone that it identifies the action of which D1 and D2 are both descriptions. But it is identification, not deduction, that is in question here, and identifications only have to be accomplished, not proved. Once we have available the systematic concept of a configuration and its constituents and recognize human behavior as a configurational phenomenon, the problem of giving sense to "the same action as" is as commonplace and presumably nonparadoxical as the problem of giving sense to "the same object as."

The relation of D4 to D1 and D2 is quite comparable to the relation of D7 ("my only filing cabinet") to D8 ("the full drawer") and D9 ("the scratched drawer"), since D7 identifies the object of which the two descriptions, D8 and D9, are descriptions of the same part, e.g., the top drawer. (Recall the BOU contingencies.) If we want a more direct relationship, we may, in place of D7, substitute D10 ("one of the drawers of my filing cabinet"), which directly identifies the object which both D8 and D9 are descriptions of. Correspondingly, in place of D4, we could move to D11 ("one of the things Brutus did to Caesar in the Forum on the Ides of March"). The latter identifies the action which D1 and D2 are both descriptions of, though, like D10, it does not do so uniquely.

Again, the problem is no more one of uniqueness in identification (though Cohen appears to presuppose this) than it is to achieve a deductive guarantee. The problem is to secure an identification which gives a clear sense to the notion that two descriptions are descriptions of the same thing. If D11 fails here, then it would seem that neither does it make sense to say that "scratched" and "full" are descriptions of the same drawer. Beyond D10, we do not have to know in advance which drawer is involved in order to understand that it could be the same drawer. Likewise, beyond D11, we do not have to know in advance which behavior it is in order to understand that both D1 and D2 could be descriptions of it.

We may note that, just because neither D1 nor D2 is deducible from D4, it is informative to be given these descriptions following the identification accomplished by D10. "One of the things Brutus did to Caesar in the Forum was to kill him with a knife" is an informative statement about what Brutus did to Caesar in the Forum. (See the discussion in Section VI of "Being Informative.") One may guess, however, that Cohen's interest is in an identification which guarantees that D1 and D2 are descriptions of the same action. This can be done, but at the sacrifice of being informative.

We may therefore turn to our other case, involving D3 "Brutus killed Caesar with a knife in the Forum" and SA6. In our normal understanding, "Brutus killed Caesar" will be the Name of a process (hence also of an event, which will not be relevant here). Correspondingly, "with a knife," "in the Forum," "on the Ides of March," etc., will represent specifications of various Options in that process. Thus, SA3 corresponds to (1) the occurrence of that process (2) in one of its Versions (a logical necessity) in which it (3) was done with a knife and (4) was done in the Forum. It would seem to follow that if any state of affairs meets conditions (1) to (4), the same state of affairs will meet condition (1), i.e., SA1, and will meet conditions (1) to (3), i.e., SA2. Thus, D3 "Brutus killed Caesar with a knife in the Forum" identifies the action which both D1 and D2 are descriptions *of*.

This resolution requires neither a fixed, finite format for giving a "complete" description of the episode nor a reference to the episode which is secured independently of description. There is no need here to "be clear how long the unelliptical form of the sentence is. . ." because "Brutus killed Caesar" is not an elliptical way of *saying* something else. Rather, it is an incomplete representation *of* something for which a different and a more complete representation, SA3, could be given.

Two points of interest remain here. First, it sometimes happens that SA1 is a constituent of SA2. In that case, SA2 will do the job of SA3. Thus, "Brutus killed Caesar" is an incomplete version (not to be confused with Version) of "Brutus killed Caesar with a knife," and so no third description is needed. In contrast, "He shot the bear with a revolver" has no such relationship to "He pointed the gun and pulled the trigger." In this case, the relationship between SA1 and SA2 must be represented within a further state of affairs, SA3. It is, apparently, when that relationship is not taken into account that we generate such cases as "He pulled the trigger with a revolver." Configuration description and the other representational formats are ways of giving such relationships an explicit representation; "quantification over events" is not.

Second, it may not be obvious that in general the applicability of a factual Chronological description is presupposed when we say that D1 and D2 are descriptions of the same thing. But consider the case where "Brutus killed Caesar" and "Brutus killed Caesar with a knife" are given not as references to a single historical particular, but rather merely as "repeatable" Configuration descriptions. If we allow multiple instances of each description, then the resolution above is not available, for it will not in general be the case then that "Brutus killed Caesar" describes the same episode as "Brutus killed Caesar with a knife." If another Brutus killed another Caesar in the Forum by poisoning him, and we say of *that* event that "Brutus killed Caesar," this will not be an incomplete version of "Brutus killed Caesar with a knife" nor will it be a description of the same episode. The conceptual distinctions, structures, and procedures associated with the SA system provide a technical implementation of the logic of part-whole relationships; the propositional calculus and the theory of reference do not.

V

BEYOND

TECHNOLOGY AND SUPERSTITION

IN THE PRECEDING SECTION we dealt with some current problems which have more than a passing relevance for scientific thought and practice, though neither the problems nor the disciplines involved would ordinarily be thought of as "scientific." In this section it will be appropriate to give some further illustrations of the contributions which can be provided by the systematic formulation of the real world and its representation, this time dealing with issues directly concerning behavioral science and scientists.

More specifically, I shall undertake two tasks here. The first is to use the state-of-affairs system as a perspective from which to examine critically the place of reductionist policies and the ideology of determinism in the behavioral sciences. The second is to provide some substantive backing for the claim that in fact there is a point in not keeping the methodological, substantive, and historical aspects of behavioral science in the traditional logic-tight compartments. Primarily this is done by illustrating a "substantive" way of dealing with a supposedly "methodological" issue (determinism again) and a "methodological" way of dealing with a supposedly "substantive" issue (the self-concept). More accurately, what is illustrated is a reality-oriented behavioral approach in which both "substantive" and "methodological" resources are freely available in descriptive and explanatory constructions.

89

A third task, addressed in the final section, is to give some explicit delineation of the form which a behavioral science might take, considering that "the real world" is, substantively, what that behavioral science is about. Since the social institution of science is one in which the relationships among linguistic behavior, non-linguistic behavior, and the real world are crucial, it is inevitable that the delineation of this possibility on the basis of only the "real world" portion of the Person Concept will be appreciably incomplete. However, even this much of a suggestion is nontrivial in that acting on it would involve doing some things differently in the practice of behavioral science. Moreover, given the technical resources presented in Sections II and III, it is something that could actually happen, now. So there is a point in talking that way.

A.   How Not to Reify Biological and Physical Concepts

It has long seemed obvious, in our pictorially oriented empiricism, that nations are "nothing over and above" their citizens, that each citizen is "nothing over and above" his physiological structures, that those physiological structures are nothing over and above et ceteras, and in the end, there is nothing over and above the hypothetical ultimate particles which the physicists talk about. Historically, the reductionist "nothing but" approach has predominated in the customary verbal and nonverbal practices of behavioral science. One expression of this predominance is the widespread denial that any behavioral description could be a fundamental description, for all behavioral *attributions*, it is said, are really inferences based on something more fundamental than behavior, e.g., movements, "perceptual cues," or statistical covariation data.

Reductionism has predominated not in the form of a substantive thesis which would be empirically vulnerable, but rather as a pre-empirical policy, which is perhaps only politically vulnerable. As an established policy it has a normative force and not merely a numerical predominance; reductive and atomistic approaches are generally accepted as paradigms of scientific rigor. The question "Where in the causal sequence is there a place for volition to enter in and influence the course of physiological events?" provides a succinct expression of the methodological priority given to physiological facts as against behavioral facts in our substantive "explanations" of behavior.

Correspondingly, the holist, however partially successful his defense of a holistic approach has been, has always been on the defensive. But consider the following dialogue:

Wil: Oh, I admit that people, tables, mountains, and all those parochially middle-sized things you laymen and behavioral scientists like to talk about are real. But they're real only because they're made up of little things, Zilch particles, and those little things are what are *really* real.

Gil: Rubbish! You've got it exactly backwards. Those hypothetical little things you talk about—if you insist on conjuring up such things and calling them real, I won't say they aren't, but if they are, it's only because they're parts of a *big* thing, the real world, and that's what's *really* real.

The state-of-affairs system formulation shows the detailed basis for the symmetry in this exchange. The basis lies in (a) configurational composition and decomposition and (b) LC-I and LC-II. Specifically, Wil chooses to define his ultimates by recourse to LC-II and views other objects as compositions; Gil chooses LC-I as the ultimate and views other objects as decompositions. With respect to world formulas generated by the Transition Rules and limiting cases, either choice is formally available. However, since Gil's ultimate has the advantage of being observable and guaranteed real (recall the relation of observation and reality to the Chronological description) as contrasted with the unobservable and hypothetical particles of Wil, one might wonder why the holistic approach has not been predominant.

Part of the reason appears to be that a simple, straightforward statement such as that presented by Gil has not been generally available. We noted in Section IV that Gruner's formulation, being merely relativistic and not calculational, makes it necessary to replace one description with another rather than using one description to enrich another. In turn, that makes it impossible to say, for example, that both the nation and its citizens are objects; and so it seems that one has to make a choice—is it the nation or the citizen that is the *real* object here?

A similar difficulty has been at work, historically, in regard to LC-I and smaller objects. It has appeared to philosophers that if the real world is conceived as an object via appeal to LC-I then that requires that individual persons (and a fortiori, Zilch particles) be thought of as *states* of that object. Thus, one finds a quite recent philosophical comment to the effect that of course one could refer to the existence of Jane Parker by saying that the universe took on a Jane Parkerish tinge for a while, but really that would be rather too barbaric. And so it would, and it would be incorrect as well.

The State-of-Affairs formulation does not, of course, require any such barbarism or involve any such error. Just as it permits us to say that the nation is an object and a citizen is another object, so we may say that the real world is an object or state of affairs of which Jane Parker is this smaller, constituent object. There is no need to talk about tinges, and we may be as precise and as detailed about it as we please. Thus, the SA system formulation clears away some merely apparent difficulties connected with a holistic approach to real-world phenomena and gives Gil at least an even break with Wil in principle.

In-principle adequacy, however, is not yet practicability, and mere practicability is something less than established and coherent practice. In practice, it is the Basic Process Unit which provides the most immediately practicable implementation of a holistic approach.

With the BPU format in mind, let us consider the statement that P-NameA1 took place here this morning. Let this statement be abbreviated as "S," and let the "Name" which is referentially interchangeable with "P-NameA1" be, say, "degradation ceremony." Thus, "S" = "A degradation ceremony took place here this morning." Ordinarily, in the reductive approach, we would take S on the semantic model of "name and object," i.e., as referring to an existing historical particular in all its concrete detail. The latter would be a particular process, and one composed, no doubt, of smaller particular processes P-NameA11, P-Name A12, . . . , P-NameA1K and their corresponding Elements (objects). On this view, we should have to say that S was a crude and possibly misleading way of talking about those smaller particulars which, if we consider both the subprocesses and their individual Elements, are what was really going on (and so on down the decompositional ladder to Zilch particles and their goings-on).

In the holistic approach, however, we do not take S as the use of the name of that *thing* (P-NameA1). Rather, we take S as providing information about the world, and specifically, about some part and some aspect of it (S is a Chronological description). S is a piece of information about the world because it is a partial specification of a more extensive process (P-NameA) of which P-NameA1 is either a Stage-Option or a Version (to designate it as P-NameA1 is to indicate the former). To say that P-NameA1 occurred is to

93

provide the information that P-NameA occurred in *this* one of the ways (Versions) in which it could have occurred. But, of course, that information is, in turn, simply the information that an even more extensive process occurred in *this* one (P-NameA) of the ways in which *it* could have occurred (and so on up the compositional ladder to LC-I). To be sure, S may be a poor, or even misleading, way of conveying that information, since S does not *say* that P-NameA occurred. But if we cannot give or imply a particular more extensive process, LC-I is always available and we can give a Chronological description or simply note that our description is incomplete. In effect, then, either a statement, S, or an observation, S, functions not as a name but as a constraint (a reality constraint) on acceptable world formulas and descriptions. S partitions logical space into those world descriptions which are compatible with it and those which are not. Given S, we restrict our world descriptions to the former and reject the latter. This feature is retained as we come down the decompositional ladder from LC-I to S to talking about Zilch particles. The latter are not ultimate building blocks but rather "the last decimal place" in the detail with which we specify LC-I. Thus, to say that a degradation ceremony took place here this morning is to say that the history of the group and the history of the world took a particular course here this morning. In this way, none of our "referents" is reified.

Note that neither Wil's reductionism nor Gil's holism tells him what the real world is like. Both must make the necessary observations, and the problem of relating S "upward" to P-NameA and "downward" to P-NameA1K is present in both cases. Let us survey a particular example briefly.

The reference to volition, above, was not invented. More than fifteen years after both Ryle's *Concept of Mind* and Wittgenstein's *Philosophical Investigations* (for example) it is possible to find in the psychological journals such a question as "At what point in the causal sequence of physiological events does volition enter in to affect behavior?" along with the suggestion that since experimental psychologists have largely neglected the problem it most likely is at least partly a merely verbal one.

Gil's short and polemic answer to this question is "Nonsense! In 'the world of physiology' there are no such possible facts involving volition—by definition." It is not literally a definition that is involved here but rather a case of Contingency 4b(2)C in the Basic Object Unit, i.e., a commitment to use certain terminology in certain places only if certain other terminology is used in certain other places. That is, in short, a commitment to use a certain vocabulary, and perhaps a certain conceptual system, in giving descriptions over the range of phenomena to which it is applicable.

Consider some of the possibilities which are codified by Contingency 4b(2)C. Suppose, for example, that there was in current use a portion of our behavioral vocabulary which had a term-for-term correspondence to our physiological (and biochemical, etc.) vocabularies in regard to meaning, observational basis, and use, but with the contingency that the applicability of this terminology presupposed that the referents were constituents of larger, human objects. Our understanding of human behavior, i.e., Configurations involving human objects as constituents, would include what we now refer to as "physiology," "genetics," etc. And then we might well ask "At what point in the behavioral structure of events do physiological processes enter in to affect behavior? Aren't they really epiphenomenal, when you come right down to it?" And so they would be—given *that* behavioral choice of descriptive commitment.

To the unwilling ear, this example will quite possibly sound farfetched. But one could argue that we already have such a vocabulary, i.e., the one we call "physiological." And one could argue along two complementary lines here.

(a) Nobody supposes that the action of muscles, bones, and nerves "influences" human behavior unless these various objects are parts of a living, behaving human being. That is to say, that part-whole relationship is presupposed when "physiological" states of affairs are used to "explain" human behavior. But since human behavior is a process, a human body and its constituents are Elements in such processes and the processes involving those constituents will be constituent processes in the more extensive behavioral processes. *Pace* Gruner, the relation between a process and its subprocesses is neither causal nor deductive; it is, rather, the part-whole relationship which is codified by the Transition Rules and the concepts of composition and decomposition. When we describe human objects or human behavior in the degree of three-dimensional topographic detail which involves reference to such body units as muscles, bones, and nerves, we introduce, via decomposition, a new set of Stage-Options and Elements, together with the formal possibility of new Contingency specifications which elaborate our descriptions of behavioral possibilities.

To be sure, physiological characterization is only *a* way of talking about human beings, since it represents only a particular (predictive-manipulatively oriented) sort of O-Paradigm, or immediate constituent analysis, of human bodies; but it *is* a way of talking about human beings, even though that fact is not within the scope of the world of physiology.

(b) When a systematic technical vocabulary is used, we cannot tell from that fact alone what commitments are carried therewith (just as from the occurrence of the degradation ceremony alone we could not tell what more extensive process it was a Version of, and just as from an inspection of "It is certain that P" we could not tell what the methodological status of this declaration was). In point of fact, it appears that the use of physiological and other technical vocabularies is highly equivocal in this regard.

When physiological terminology is used to "explain" something about human behavior, the commitment is that the reference is to constituents of living, behaving human objects. (This is the case (a), above.) On the other hand, when the same vocabulary is used in the course of the professional physiological practice of description, theorizing, or experimentation, the commitment is to the exclusive use of that technical vocabulary over its range of application. And since "human behavior" does not fall within that range, because it has no conceptual locus and therefore no factual locus within "the world of physiology," no putative explanations of human behavior can be given when the vocabulary is used as a technical physiological vocabulary.

The distinction between the two commitments is generally not made, even though the two are incompatible in that they could not be fulfilled simultaneously. The confusion between the two is comparable to supposing that if I buy a chess set or make one out of ivory then my behavior is explained by the rules of chess which define "the world of chess" or that if I count my change at the grocery store my behavior is explained by a set of rules for the axiomatization of arithmetic. (There is, in fact, a sense in which one could speak of an "explanation" here and that sense is systematically derivable as an "Achievement Description" within the behavior-descriptive portion (Ossorio, 1969a, 1973) of the Person Concept.) In short, the error underlying the equivocation is to suppose that the fact that we use a term of art such as "neurone," "reinforcement," "pawn," or "square root" to *identify or designate* some object, process, event, or state of affairs or attribute commits us to the ideology of the professional practices within which the term first evolved.

Since commitments regarding the use of a given vocabulary or conceptual system have nothing per se to do with truth or falsity, there does not appear to be any generally nontrivial question of the form "Is it true that human beings are physiological objects?" or "Is human behavior really a physiological process?" A fortiori, there is no empirical question of this sort, nor is it the case that scientists have *discovered* that human beings are physiological objects. (That the human beings we are familiar with have hearts, basal ganglia, and carbohydrate metabolism was an empirical discovery, but had those findings been different, *that* would still be physiology.)

But, if the traditional empiricism formally fails us here, the new empiricism does not. This is the very kind of situation in which it is clear that the question to ask is not "It is true?" but rather "Is there a point in talking that way?" Since Wil and Gil provide us with paradigms, the answer is "yes" for both ways of talking. We move then to the next elaboration, i.e, "*When* is there a point in talking that way, and *what* is the point then?"

In this connection we may return briefly to the historical, methodological, and substantive aspects of science. Since behavioral scientists as a matter of historical fact frequently and routinely talk about behavior in physiological terms or give physiological concepts theoretical or methodological priority over behavioral concepts, there is *that* point in talking that way, i.e., one is following the current custom of the profession. In this sense, the science of behavior is whatever behavioral scientists say it is and whatever they do in their role as behavioral scientists. The latter tack is the one generally taken by philosophers of science with respect to the "natural" sciences.

For the present, we may pass such considerations by as belonging to the politics of science rather than the practice of science per se, noting only that there is such a point and that the scientific behavior of scientists may be highly predictable from a knowledge of such facts. If we ask "When is there a point in using the physiological vocabulary to formulate behavioral facts if one's purpose is to maximize our understanding of behavior," we can give the partial answer stemming from (a) above: There is a point in going to that level of detail when it permits us to formulate behaviorally significant Contingencies (states of affairs) in our (Configuration description) representations of behavior.

In this way the new empiricism provides a guideline for how to have a behavioral science which (a) has a place, substantively and methodologically, for all behaviorally relevant facts, including findings generated by "outsiders" such as laymen, theologians, physiologists, and biochemists, (b) without reifying nonbehavioral concepts as "the real thing" and so forfeiting, in any but a political sense, its character as *behavioral* science and as behavioral *science*.

So far we have considered cases in which it is presupposed that Wil's Zilch particles (or processes, etc.), be they physiological, physical, or whatnot, are constituents of the human objects and behaviors which they are purported to cause. It should be clear that the restriction to human objects and behaviors is in no way essential except when facts concerning human objects and behaviors are what is to be "explained." Thus, Wil does not have a counterargument to the effect that Zilch particles follow laws of their own whether they are parts of human objects or not. For wherever a Zilch particle may be found (or better, *supposed*) to be following its laws, it will be part of some larger object and state of affairs. So the lawfulness of Zilch particles cannot be divorced from their constituency in the very objects and states of affairs which they are commonly and zealously purported to explain.

Given the mirror-image similarity shown above between the ways the holistic and reductive approaches were implemented, I suggested that part of the explanation for the predominance of a reductive policy is that a simple and explicit statement of the symmetry has not been generally available. However, apparently promising approaches are not generally neglected just because they cannot be shown to be sound in advance. Other historical deterrents to holism have been present. Chief among those has been what can best be described as "the prevailing scientific ideology," though that will strike many as an unduly polemic characterization and diagnosis. Two major elements of this ideology are determinism and the unity of the sciences. The first of these is dealt with below; a brief examination of the "unity" notion will be to the point here.

It has always been clear, in modern times at least, that the real world is all of one piece. In contrast, the scientific study of the world is divided into a small, but various, set of distinct sciences, or scientific enterprises. Though they all appeal to a common set of "methodological principles," they in fact produce a variety of distinct theories and explanations. It has been an article of scientific faith that "ultimately" these various accounts will be assimilated into one scientific account of one real world. Since the "ultimate" phenomena of the various sciences correspond to their basic explanatory concepts, and since the explanatory concepts in the various sciences do not form any single conceptual system, the possibilities for unification are limited.

If the ultimate phenomena of the various sciences were to remain as conceptual ingredients in the "unified" account, then clearly that account could not be provided by any of the existing sciences or by any new science modeled thereon, for no such science could encompass the concepts of any other science. But in that case, our faith in unification would be mistaken; for in that case it would follow that no single *scientific* account of the real world was possible, though an integration of scientific accounts might still be accomplished, say, by philosophers, theologians, or historians.

The alternative is to adopt one of the sciences as the touchstone, as the fundamental science, and show that the concepts and explanatory accounts given by other sciences could in some sense be reduced to or derived from the fundamental science. It is this alternative which provides the motivation for Wil's statement that those big things are "nothing but" those little things and for the experimental psychologist's bland assertion that references to "volition" are merely expressions of the layman's ignorance of neurophysiology.

One of the more recent and "enlightened" versions of the unity theme is stated in terms of "levels of organization." It is enlightened in that in this version it is denied that phenomena (e.g., nations) are *simply* nothing but smaller phenomena (e.g., citizens). The unity is provided by the fact that the phenomena of the various sciences involve the same material objects; the difference lies in that the objects of one sort are organizations of objects of a different sort. Thus, we have an arrangement that is an informal or crude version of the composition and decomposition of objects in the BOU format.

But this "enlightened" version of the unity viewpoint eschews a crude reduction of large objects to smaller ones only to replace it with an equally crude reduction of large processes to smaller ones. The crucial slogan which is common to all the well-known versions of the "levels of organization" view is that "Lawfulness at a given level of organization *depends on* lawfulness at the next lower level." Thus, behavioral lawfulness presupposes physiological lawfulness; the latter presupposes genetic lawfulness; . . . ; and in the end, it is the lawfulness of Zilch particles which, like Atlas, carries the burden of the whole world. The underlying picture is, of course, the picture of Zilch particles as the ultimate *stuff* of which everything else *must be* composed or arranged; and the underlying principle is that if something is so that is because something else (ultimately Zilch-particulate dynamics) makes it so. The notion that Zilch particles are what there really is is easily convertible into the alternate form, i.e., that Zilch processes are what really happen.

But since the real world, as LC-I, does not unroll through time and since it could not possibly require anything to bring it or any of its parts into existence, Gil's direct response to the "enlightened" view would again be "Rubbish!"

More specifically, and with the Basic Process Unit in mind, it may be recalled that the occurrence of a process having multiple Versions neither implies nor presupposes the occurrence of any particular one of those Versions. The occurrence of P-NameA neither implies nor presupposes the occurrence of Stage-Option P-NameA13 if there are other options P-NameA11, P-NameA12, ..., et cetera. This is so both for a single occurrence of P-NameA or for the regular occurrence of P-NameA within some larger process (with the regularity being represented by a Contingency specification within a Configuration description of that larger process).

Thus, it follows that lawfulness at a given "level of organization" *in no way* depends on any *independent* lawfulness at any "lower" level, nor could any "lower level" lawfulness in any way guarantee any "higher level" lawfulness. If a given process, P-NameA, occurs at all, it occurs in one of the ways in which it can occur, and no account whatever of regularities or irregularities at lower levels of organization will have any bearing on the matter. To put it in a familiar context, if a given physiological theory, no matter how rigorously backed up by experimental data, were to imply that the behavior which we observe could not occur, that physiological theory would be ipso facto false (of course physiological theories are not vulnerable to this kind of evidence because they have no such implications). Conversely, if physiologists had discovered only a chaotic and irregularly distributed set of structures and processes in people's heads, we should not on that account conclude that people didn't really feel and think or that the behavioral regularities which we see around us were an illusion.

If there are any simple connections between "levels" such that, for example, P-NameA could only occur in one of two Versions,

P-NameA11 or P-NameA12, then to that degree the occurrence of P-NameA forces regularity on the lower level; for then it determines that either P-NameA11 or P-Name A12 occurred, and not the other way around (recall that the occurrence of a process does not imply the occurrence of any given one of the more extensive processes of which it could be a constituent). Correspondingly, if P-NameA were prevented from occurring, so would either of its Versions be prevented from occurring, so that once more it is the higher level happening which takes precedence.

In short, though enlightenment comes in various versions, the "levels of organization" version of unity is not one of them.

Even more recently than the "levels of organization" view, the reductionistic policy in behavioral explanation is exemplified by a variety of "Identity Hypotheses." A hypothesis of this sort asserts that *as a matter of fact* mental processes are identical with brain processes. Thus, for example, experiencing the redness of an after-image is a process which, though it is a mental process by definition, is a physiological process as a matter of fact; so also is thinking of eating pickles, or feeling sorry for the losing team.

The principal basis for the plausibility of such assertions is the suggestion that the mentalistic description is a noncommittal, or indefinite, description which only identifies its referent in a more or less vague fashion but gives no information as to the nature and characteristics of that referent. Thus, "the thought of eating pickles" is uninformative in the way that "what's going on in the next room" and "Jack's misfortune" are uninformative. That is, just as the one tells us nothing about what it is that Jack's misfortune is, and the other tells us nothing about what it is that is going on in the next room, the first tells us nothing about what it is that is going on in the brain of the person doing the thinking.

Since the Transition Rules of Section II are rules for preserving real-world identity across different forms of representation, the concepts introduced in Sections II and III should have some relevance to these Identity Hypotheses. Indeed, the issues here bear a strong resemblance to those involved in the problem of descriptions of the same action, though they are not the same. Consider the following statements:

S1   Brutus killed Caesar.
S2   Brutus killed Caesar with a knife.
S3   I'm thinking of eating pickles.
S4   I'm having a discharge through neural circuit X-301.

Note that although it has been suggested that S1 is an elliptical form of S2, no such suggestion is possible with respect to S3 and S4, for S3 and S4 do not overlap at all in what they say. Thus, the only possible correspondence between S3 and S4 that would be of any interest is that with S3 and S4 we are talking about the same thing, even though we are not saying the same thing about it. The double standard embodied in the reductionist policy in behavioral explanation is shown in the fact that, instead of saying that S3 and S4 have the same referent, the Identity thesis is that the brain process mentioned in S4 *is* the referent. (So that Gil could say to Wil for openers, "Nonsense! Talking about that live circuit is simply a technician's superstitious way of talking about the thought of eating pickles.")

We may use the BPU notation to represent some possible states of affairs in a neutral way. Specifically, we shall want three "levels" of process representation:

P-NameA   "ordering lunch"
P-NameA1   "thinking of eating pickles"
P-NameA11,   P-NameA12, . . . , P-Name A1K
P-NameA1K

104

Thus, P-NameA is some process which, for purposes of our example, is the behavioral process of ordering lunch. P-NameA1 is one of the stages in that process, and in our example it is the "mental process" of thinking about eating pickles. The third line represents a sequence of subprocesses which make up one Version of P-NameA1. For convenience, this sequence is abbreviated as P-NameA1K.

Given this notation, we may now raise some questions about the three processes and their relationships and about which process a given description is a description of and which process a given description can be used to talk about or give information about.

Our first question will be: Suppose that we introduce "Activation of brain circuit X-301" as the Name of a process and let the Description of that process be given as a sequence of stages with no options (i.e., we are dealing with only one Version here) and as a sequence in which all the Individuals and Elements are specified in "physiological" terminology. This process is now a candidate for the status of the process designated as P-NameA1K, above. Thus, if the mention of P-NameA1 is a way of referring to P-NameA1K and "I'm thinking of eating pickles" is that mention, then we have apparently shown how the reference to a mental process can be a case of referring to a process which is the same process as a physiological process.

Note, however, that Gil might object to such a move and appeal to LC-III. For he might claim that the examples of "Jack's misfortune" and "something going on in the next room," although they serve to clarify the nature of the Identity thesis, also show what is wrong with it. Misfortunes and goings-on in the next room cannot just happen *that* way. If they happen at all they happen as financial losses, physical injuries et al., and as card parties, Sunday dinners, family arguments et al. In contrast, thinking about eating pickles is not obviously something that couldn't just happen that way. It is not obvious that if it happens at all it must happen in a more particular way. And if, on examination, it appeared that it did, then the particulars would be of an equally mental sort, e.g., imagining a pickle, imagining biting into it, thinking how good it tasted, etc. Thus, we would in this way generate another candidate for the status of the process designated as P-NameA1K, above, and this candidate would be a mental process.

But now, by a symmetrical move upward, it is clear that we could give a Process description having the form of P-NameA1 but one in which once more the Elements and Individuals could be specified in physiological terms. Evidently the only case of interest here is the first one where we consider P-NameA1 as a mental process and P-NameA1K, if not literally as a physiological process, at least susceptible of a specification in physiological language. The reason for this is that where we suppose the same process formula in both physiological and mentalistic terms (a) it will simply be the case discussed previously, where one may choose language which carries different commitments; (b) there will be no question of one of the descriptions being technically deficient, yet the current Identity theses stress the asymmetry in the technical adequacy of the mentalistic and physiological descriptions; and (c) some existing counterarguments would then apply, i.e., arguments to the effect that identity would be indistinguishable from co-occurrence and the so-called Identity thesis would be only a verbal imposture covering the traditional views of psychophysical parallelism or "double language" views.

The remaining case, where P-NameA1 is the mental process and P-NameA1K is the physiological process, has some additional interest because it would seem that mental processes cannot be decomposed indefinitely (unless we appeal to LC-IV and talk about a continuous process in which nothing changes), whereas bodies, whether human or physiological, can, at least practically speaking. So our remaining case is one which would arise when we have decomposed the mental process into some ultimate constituents. As it happens, we have a familiar example of this kind of relationship in the case of a computer "doing arithmetic." Elementary arithmetic operations set a lower bound to the fineness with which we can represent its "mental process" of "doing arithmetic"; and, although over some range there will be parallel electronic and arithmetic descriptions of what the computer is doing, there will also be a range where only electronic Process descriptions can be given; for a complex series of such processes may correspond to the elementary arithmetic operation of "adding one."

Given this paradigm setting for a possible Identity thesis, we may find the logical basis for such a thesis in the relation between a process and one of its Versions. In the presentation of the Basic Process Unit, I said that the occurrence of a process on a given occasion is the occurrence of one of its Versions on that occasion, and this does sound like an Identity thesis of some kind. Note, however, that this condition is compatible with any of the following states of affairs.

SA1. Although P-NameA1 occurs frequently, no Version of P-NameA1 occurs more than once, and no Version of P-NameA1 resembles any other Version in any respect other than in being a Version of P-NameA1.

SA2. There is no way of distinguishing one particular Version from another.

SA3. There is an infinite set of possible Versions and no way of setting a limit to the kind or number of them that could actually happen.

SA4. There are N Versions, N being a small, finite number, and the occurrences of the different Versions on different occasions have a more or less regular distribution across the N possibilities, but the distribution varies from person to person, from population to population, and for the same person over long intervals of time.

SA5. There is no Version which could not possibly be deliberately brought about by the person whose behavior or mental process is P-NameA1.

SA6. There are N Versions of P-NameA1, and the distribution of occurrences of Versions across the N possibilities is stable over persons, populations, and time.

SA7. There is only one Version of P-NameA1, namely, P-Name-A1K, but the latter may occur without the occurrence of P-NameA1.

SA8. There is only one Version of P-NameA1, namely, P-Name-A1K, and one occurs if, and only if, the other does.

Among these possibilities, we shall see that only SA8 leaves room for an Identity thesis. We may eliminate SA6 on the grounds that we would then be committed to saying that P-NameA1 was identical to several things which were not identical to one another; and, if we went to this length to protect an Identity thesis, we should lose not only the Identity thesis, but also the concepts of identity and thesis themselves. The same consideration holds for SA1 to SA5, all of which allow for various Versions actually occurring; moreover, under any of the conditions SA1–SA5 it would seem that any assertion of identity between P-NameA1 and any Version would be empty and misleading rhetoric.

We may eliminate SA7 on the same grounds as SA6. For SA7 may be paraphrased as saying that P-NameA1K is sometimes identical to P-NameA1 and sometimes identical to Non-P-NameA1. This is a technical deficit which can be remedied, however. For in the case of SA7 we should have to suppose that there is some set of conditions, X, such that P-NameA1 was identical to P-NameA1K if and only if X. But that would be to say that P-NameA1 was identical to P-NameA1K plus X. That, however, is just a variant of SA8.

SA8, moreover, has the virtue of being logically possible without being logically necessary. However, it is not the kind of statement which could be refuted or demonstrated by any set of observational results, and in this respect it resembles a scientific theory or hypothesis, not a prediction. For no matter what we observed, if we found a common element that finding might not hold up; and if we did not find a common element, well, who knows but what someday, with more powerful experimental or verbal technology, we might. Evidently, the Identity thesis is not an empirical guess about how the world is, but rather a preempirical policy: "Treat behavior and mental processes as though they were nothing but some physiological process and see how long and how well you can get away with it."

What *would* we be pretending was the case here? *Does* it make any sense to say, when P-NameA1 occurs in Version P-NameA1K, that P-NameA1 is identical to a state of affairs, PSA-NameA1, which has the processes P-NameA1K as its constituents? Note that there is a straightforward identity between P-NameA1 and PSA-NameA1 (by Rule 5) but not between either of them and the processes P-NameA1K.

Now, if the processes P-NameA1K were related to one another in the requisite way, then not the processes per se, but *their being so related* would be a state of affairs identical to PSA-NameA1 (by Rule 5). But that would be a conceptual truth, not a mere matter of fact What would be a mere matter of fact would be (a) that processes P-NameA1K occurred and (b) that their occurrences were properly related to one another. Here we may refer back to the "technical deficit" in SA7. The processes P-NameA1K could occur

109

without the occurrences of P-NameA1, because unless they occurred in the proper relationship P-NameA1 would not occur. Thus, the additional condition X, such that X plus P-NameA1K is identical to P-NameA1 (via the identity to PSA-NameA1), is simply (b), above, i.e., that these processes occur in the requisite relation to one another.

So we reach much the same conclusion as in the case of "Brutus killed Caesar." Insofar as S3 and S4 may be said to be different descriptions of the same process, S3 is not a defective description of a process of which S4 is a nondefective description. And nor is there any transcendental description or observational perspective or experimental device which could somehow give us direct access to *the* process of which S3 and S4 are descriptions.

Recall that in the case of "Brutus killed Caesar" we got around this impossibility by introducing a third description which was a more complete description of "the same event" in the sense that it identified a state of affairs which had as constituents the two states of affairs corresponding to S1 and S2. We noted there that the third description is essential in formulating the general case because it is indispensable in the case where one of the two descriptions is not simply a less complete version of the other.

In the present case we arrive at a similar result, but one which points up an ambiguity in the reference above to a "more complete" description. For, if there is to be a description of a process such that S3 and S4 are both descriptions of that process, that process will be P-NameA (another point for Gil). The descriptions of P-NameA1 and of P-NameA1K are both ways of (partly) specifying which Version of P-NameA took place on that occasion. So P-NameA is what both S3 and S4 can be used to say something about. And P-NameA is "more complete" in that it refers to the entire process of which P-NameA1 and P-NameA1K refer to only one stage. (Note that we could generate the previous case of "more complete" by incorporating both S3 and S4 in our description of P-NameA and adding the mention of P-NameA2, P-NameA3, etc. The latter are the analogues of adding "with a knife on the Ides of March" to "Brutus killed Caesar.")

Since it does not appear to be possible to state a coherent Identity thesis, we may ask, in the empirical tradition, what does the identity theorist expect to observe? If we do this, we are back to SA8. He expects to observe that whenever anyone thinks of eating pickles circuit X-301 is active and there is no other circuit that stands in this relation to thinking of pickles. But this is exactly what the proponents of psychophysical parallelism and epiphenomenalism would expect to find. Well, certainly the identity theorist takes himself to be making a different, and more daring, postulate than the parallelism theorist. He doesn't *mean* merely parallelism. And thinking that there is an identity is not the same mental process as thinking that there is a correspondence. But thinking so doesn't make it so, and so we might do some justice to the facts here by introducing a second-order Identity thesis. That is, the current versions of the Identity thesis are, *as a matter of fact*, identical to a non-Identity thesis.

We have, of course, in no way exhausted the difficulties which could be raised in connection with reductionism and Identity theses. But, also, in considering reductionism on its own merits we have failed to do it justice; for it does not stand on its own merits but rather gains the force that it has only in connection with the remainder of the traditional scientific ideology and, particularly, with the "deterministic" aspect of that ideology. If it were merely a question of greater or lesser detail in description or of choice of conceptual systems or choice of commitments, it seems likely that even a reductionistic bias would hardly lead behavioral scientists to adopt as a first principle the impossibility and nonintelligibility of a behavioral science. I do not think this is too strong a characterization. If behavior is really something else and depends completely or fundamentally on nonbehavioral principles, then any so-called science of behavior could only consist in showing *that* behavior is epiphenomenal and that behavioral regularities are simply derivative consequences of nonbehavioral regularities. If we are tempted to call that a science of behavior, we have only to look across the aisle to physics and ask ourselves whether we would call physics a science if that were the tack taken there.

The motivation for this self-destructive behavior is provided by the view that certain descriptions (of a Zilch-particulate sort) give us a privileged access to the mechanical principles upon which the world, being a gigantic machine, *really* operates. For, if the fate of every Zilch particle is foreordained, then everything that happens happens by virtue of its Zilch constituents, hence *in principle* the study of Zilch particles is the key to everything that happens, including behavior, and correspondingly every other topic of study in principle futile; for we can there study at most the consequences of Zilch processes under a variety of more or less naive and misleading descriptions. Here is motivation sufficient and to spare, and so we shall not avoid an examination of that topic in the next section.

At this point, a reminder may be in order. What I have done in the examination of reductionism and identity, and what I shall be doing, is to illustrate how, though the state-of-affairs formulation does not assert anything, it does provide a range of conceptual and notational resources which can be used in a variety of ways, including both the critical examination of some fundamental issues concerning behavioral science and the creative and empirically oriented formulation of behavioral phenomena. Another person using the same concepts and dealing with the same topics would doubtless proceed differently. I have not (nor shall I) take a "scholarly" approach here. That is, I have not cited particular proponents and varieties of reductionism and identity; I have not dealt with these topics in the depth or scope that is entirely feasible in principle; and I have not attempted to marshall a conclusive set of reasons for drawing particular conclusions. This is not just a matter of making do. On the contrary, it may be suggested that although a scholarly treatment has some practical value as a compendium of what people say, it is in principle inadequate.

Just as we have long seen what is naive about seeking "crucial experiments" to decide among theories which are inherently immune to falsification and can always be protected by their adherents against embarrassing facts, so we might view the notion of a single, decisive argument with respect to reductionism, determinism, and other perennial academic indoor sports. There is no limit to the variations, ad hoc qualifications, studied ignorance, and other maneuvers of which an ingenious person might avail himself by way of saving a given verbal formula, and there is no point in trying to anticipate them all. One can only be illustrative here. If there is a moral to the foregoing, it is that the kind of symmetry there is between holistic and reductive possibilities of commitment is clearly *shown* by the state-of-affairs formulation, though it is not asserted there in any particular form. A behavioral scientist who sees that symmetry clearly will have that much more freedom to pursue the study of behavior in ways which are intellectually responsive to real-world observation and conceptual coherence rather than emotionally steered by a received ideology, and he will not be easily imposed upon by a range of superstitions such as reductionism and determinism which have been pronounced to be, and until recently generally accepted as, the methodological requirements of scientific rigor in the study of behavior.

So far, it is the symmetry of composition and decomposition of objects and processes which has been emphasized. The force of the preceding illustrations is that a reductive or atomistic approach does not carry with it inherent advantages of precision, differentiation, operationalizability, quantifiability, empirical openness, or any other advantage whatever. However, I do not mean to suggest that the choice of one or the other is of no consequence. On the contrary, the final section deals with a decisive asymmetry in the composition and decomposition of states of affairs which requires an autonomous, holistic behavioral science for its conceptual and empirical elucidation.

B. Cause and Effect without Theology and Egocentricism

As we noted in Section II, the state-of-affairs system generates descriptive formulas ranging in complexity from world history to "Here is X." In general, the simpler the formula we use, the more we have confidence, prior to any observation, that we will be able to give a description that fits that formula under any circumstances whatever. "Here is a case of X" is a formula which has a cast-iron, money-back guarantee in this respect, since there is no situation in which a description having that form will not be available. The temporal succession formula "B, thereafter A" and the cause-effect formula "C, consequently E" are just noticeably less simple than "Here is a case of X," and these too have a guarantee of applicability. Note that here "applicable" amounts to "intelligible" rather than "correct," which is to say that one can always give a description of this sort without being nonsensical, and that reflects the nature of these formulas and of the concept of a "world formula." Correctness and incorrectness of descriptions, on the other hand, presuppose human standards and human practices, for only by reference to these in addition could a description be designated as true or false, correct or incorrect.

Of course, what we substitute for "C" and "E" here may be of any degree of complexity. What is simple is the formula, not necessarily the actual description or the state of affairs which is referred

114

to. For example, in the case of "The depression of the early 30's caused the landslide vote for Franklin Roosevelt in 1936," both the formula and the description are simple, whereas the state of affairs is so complex that it has never been adequately delineated. In terms of the representational resources developed in Section III, the description is a State-of-Affairs description; and it represents a state of affairs having as constituents two states of affairs, SA1 and SA2, in a temporal relation. The two constituent states of affairs are each identified by a Name without any accompanying Description (this permits a simple verbal reference to a complex state of affairs), though each Name carries some information which would be relevant to a Description. Finally, of the two constituent states of affairs, SA1 is designated as "C" and SA2 is designated as "E" in the cause-effect formula.

Of course, the real world does not per se correspond to a C-E formula any more than the English language corresponds to any particular type of sentence. On the contrary, the closest heuristic approximation to LC-I is the atemporal, aspatial, four dimensional space-time matrix of the physicist. (That world does not change through time, nor does it exist *in* space.) If we expand the s-t matrix by an indefinitely large number of additional dimensions which represent relationships other than spatiotemporal ones, that will be a *pictorial* approximation of LC-I.

Thus, the C-E formula does not have any special validity in regard to the representation of the real world. Pictorially speaking, we do not have to read LC-I from left to right in C-E form, though we can choose to do it that way. We can also read it from left to right in B-A form. And we can read it from right to left in teleological form or in A-B form, or from top to bottom or by alternate segments or Chinese box patterns or in cumulative increments from inside out in degree-of-completion form (recall Whorf's celebrated analysis of Navaho) or in any way whatever. All of these would have

115

equal validity in regard to providing representation of the real world, and all of them would be equally deficient, since none of these formulas is a possible "world formula" or even comes close for the world we know.

The nature of the deficit is perhaps best portrayed by referring to the contrast between representational ingredients and representational products and using some familiar examples. It is a well-known fact, embodied originally in the pointilliste school of art and more recently in the technology of newspaper photography and television, that one can produce a representation (on a canvas, newsprint, or cathode ray tube) of, say, a horse jumping over a fence, using only a finite set of dots varying only in their placement and in either their darkness or their area or both. We may contrast the product, i.e., the actual representation of the horse jumping over the fence, with the ingredients, i.e., the dots, which were used in that product. In such an example we can see clearly the abysmal gap between (a) the fact that a person can use the dots to produce a representation of a horse jumping over a fence and (b) the claim that dots *are* a representation of a horse jumping over a fence or the claim that since (a), then the phenomenon of a horse jumping over a fence is essentially dot-like.

The formula "use dots" in constructing representations is the analogue of using the descriptive formula "Here is an X." The analogue of "C-E" would be something like "Every dot must have an adjacent dot" or "After every dot, make another." Such a formula can indeed be *used* by a person in constructing a representation of a horse jumping over a fence. But the formula as such not only is not itself a representation of a horse jumping over a fence, but it is not even a formula *for* constructing such a representation. That is, it is not a recipe which, if only one follows it, will enable one to produce a representation of a horse jumping over a fence. This is easily seen from the fact that the formula is content-free. It does

116

not change, no matter whether we are constructing a representation of a horse jumping over a fence, a pig flying over the moon, a moving finger writing on the wall, or a conversation between Wil and Gil. Likewise, the cause-effect formula does not change, no matter whether we describe a depression causing a landslide vote or a buzzing sound causing a rat to jump out of a black compartment and into a white one.

Considering the overwhelming priority given to custom and precedent in the social practices of scientists, it perhaps needs to be emphasized that although we have a tradition of giving cause-effect descriptions, cause-effect is not per se a fact, but simply a formula which can be applied, if we insist, whenever we have temporal succession. Since we can, there is no point in insisting, and in fact we do not. However, if the formula is used subject to some rational (i.e., intelligible) rule, for example, if it is used only in the case where what we call "C" is always observed to be followed by what we designate as "E," then there may be a point in talking that way. If there is, then a description (e.g., "The depression caused the landslide vote") which exemplifies the C-E formula will have a particular status. Just as "It is certain that P" exemplifies a linguistic convention for assigning a particular status to the statement that P, "C caused E" exemplifies a linguistic convention for assigning a particular status to the statement that C was followed by E.

What the particular status is will differ, depending on which convention (rule) is involved and what one's approach to the matter is. Under Carl G. Hempel's "covering law" formulation of causal accounts, to say that C caused E is to say that it was certain that C would be followed by E because it always happens that way. Under Herbert L. Hart and Antony M. Honoré's formulation it is to say that on that occasion C's being followed by E was both (a) intelligible and (b) not a matter of luck, chance, accident, or coincidence (in this regard it resembles Dray's "rationale").

Thus, although the C-E formula has no particular validity in regard to representing the real world, it does have some distinctive features and a particular status which reflects those features. Let us survey these features briefly.

First, since the C-E formula is a temporal succession formula it provides a way of mapping both the sequential structure of the stages in a process and the order in which we establish states of affairs. Hence it lends itself to predictive use and to the representation of before-after contingencies within some process structures.

Second, the C-E formula is a special case of the Means-Ends description presented in Section III. For, if C causes E, then bringing about the occurrence of C is a way of bringing about the occurrence of E, and so C is a means to E. Because of this, the C-E formula provides a way of codifying our human capabilities and potentials for bringing about particular states of affairs. As against the means-ends form, the C-E formula has the advantage of conforming to the classical impersonal idiom which is part of our verbal scientific practice and which is frequently confused with objectivity.

Upon this fact rests the premier place of The Experiment in traditional scientific practice and the ready equation of "empirical" with "experimental." It is by no means accidental that the acid test in traditional scientific practice of whether B causes A is whether an experimenter, G, can cause A by causing B. In a means-ends formulation we would preserve all of these relationships, i.e., "G brings about B, consequently A." In the traditional practices the G-B link (the experimenter and the "independent variables") is embodied in a "methodological" account. The B-A link (the independent and dependent variables) is formulated as a cause-effect phenomenon in the "theoretical" formulation and the Iron Curtain between methodological and theoretical accounts is maintained. There seems to be no public argument about the fact that experimental manipulation is taken as the criterion for causation not because experimental manipulation is taken to be a special kind of causation, but rather because it is the kind which defines our scientific interest. That is, our traditional scientific interest in the real world is not in the observable real world as such, but rather in the real world insofar as it is actually or potentially manipulable in a unilateral (G-B) way.

Third, the C-E formula is also a special case of a Task analysis. We noted in Section III the ambiguity in normal discourse in connection with Means-Ends description and Task analysis. Thus, if we have the task of accomplishing an E which we do not have the ability to accomplish directly, one way to formulate the task is as the task of finding a middle term (state of affairs) which stands as a C with respect to that E and also stands as an E with respect to some of our possible behaviors. If we succeed in this, we will be in a position to bring about C, consequently E.

To summarize our survey, the cause-effect formula has the scientific utility that it has because it can be used by human beings in a variety of ways which are intelligible and effective independently of the C-E formula itself and certainly independently of any supposedly necessary or universal connection between C and E.

Historically, the C-E formula has served to provide the logical form (and the practical ideal) of our technology (i.e., of the confident achievement of known ends by the legitimately confident recourse to known and teachable means). As I have indicated, this feature reflects the (nonempirical) fact that the C-E formula is a truncated version of a means-ends formulation, and the latter is the overt and criterial form of a technology. Earlier in the discussion we saw that the C-E formula is defective as a representation of the real world. Subsequently we saw that though it is defective from the standpoint of representation of the real world, the C-E formula does codify our traditional scientific interest in the real world, i.e., an interest in it insofar as it is actually or potentially manipulable in a unilateral way. To see the world as being *really* a gigantic machine is to see it as a set of actual or potential opportunities for exploitation. To see it that way is to reify our manipulative interest in it, and that is to see it in a way which is perhaps not so much anthropomorphic as merely egocentric.

I mention this not to suggest that there is something in principle improper about human beings pursuing human ends and doing so in a persistent and systematic way, but because seeing the extreme limitations of the C-E formula as a form of representation and seeing the egocentricity inherent in the reification and overwhelming priority given to that formula cast a certain light on two of the most honored superstitions in the history of science. The first is that a causal account within a general causal framework (traditional "naturalism") is the epitome of hardheaded, realistic, *objective* representation of the real world. The second is that the manipulative successes in both "experimental" and "applied" settings which are associated with causal scientific accounts constitute compelling evidence for the adequacy of those accounts as representations of the real world and that in the face of this success only a wishful thinker would think of rejecting the in-principle adequacy of such accounts (see, e.g., Minsky's comments, below). But we have seen what that way of thinking amounts to in considering the successful use of dots. That example, incidentally, serves to portray the general problem of the sense in which scientific theories are empirical. We use both those dots and those scientific theories successfully in certain ways—are they then not *true*? Since that success depends at least as much on the using as on the ingredients (and perhaps depends wholly on the using, in the sense that any ingredients would do) and since neither those dots nor those theories encompass the facts of their own use, the answer is "no." As I indicated earlier, the sense in which scientific theories are empirical has never been adequately explicated either by philosophical theorists or by those scientists who profess to provide us with "empirically based" theories.

The notion that a causal account within a general causal framework is the epitome of realism and objectivity has not evolved and survived in isolation. It is buttressed by the doctrine of "determinism," which functions as a theory of causality when a "covering law" interpretation of the C-E formula is adopted. Thus, briefly, under the covering law formulation, this B caused this A not necessarily because B's always cause A's but because this B is an X and this A is a Y, and X's always cause Y's. That is, the position of an X in regard to a Y is that of C to E. The "determinist" adds to this, "And there is nothing that doesn't happen that way: Every phenomenon is an A in this sense, and so everything that happens *had to* happen and nothing that happens *could have* been otherwise."

An explanatory account given in the vocabulary of a deterministic theory has, therefore, many points in common with the Chronological description presented in Section III. Indeed, it may be regarded as a special case. Recall that a Chronological description is characterized not by any distinctive form or content, but rather by the commitment to its being part of a world formula which encompasses the history of the real world. Likewise, a deterministic theoretical account is distinguished not by any distinctive form or content or other visible mark, but rather by the commitment to its being part of a world formula which encompasses the history of the real world *and is of a particular sort,* namely, one which consists of C-E links and only those.

The effect of this move is to create verbally the a priori guarantee that the real world has at least this much unity and at least this kind of order and intelligibility. (Note that LC-I carries no such guarantee.) Since the scientific enterprise is traditionally described as a search for the orderliness of Nature, it is commonly supposed

121

that the acceptance of determinism as an article of scientific faith is essential in order that the scientist's search for that orderliness be a rational behavior. Of course no such faith is necessary and no such guarantee is either necessary or possible. There can be a point in looking for orderliness so long as it is not certain that it will not be found, and it will never be certain that it will not be found. And we need not all have the same point in looking for whatever order we may find. Neither need it be the same discovered order which satisfies us.

A second effect of the deterministic move is to create a special vocabulary and a special set of entities (which I have given the abstract designation of "Zilch particles" in the earlier discussion). For the causal regularities hold only among the theoretical and hypothetical X's and Y's, not among the (usually) observable and real A's and B's. The rat's jumping into the white box when the buzzer sounds is (one would have to suppose) mysterious, but when we see the buzzer as "stimulus" and jumping as "response" it becomes intelligible, because the stimulus *causes* the response. The final step here is predictable. If the unity and orderliness of nature is a matter of the unity and orderliness of X's and Y's as contrasted with the A's and B's, then nothing in nature can be allowed to depend (*really* depend) on the A's and B's as such. Since human beings are among the A's and B's, problems arise when we try to formulate a behavioral science within a clockwork model of the real world. The traditional version of the problem is that of determinism and freedom, but in its most pertinent form it may be expressed as the problem of responsibility and truth (or knowledge).

It is frequently supposed that the problem of determinism and freedom arises from the nature of scientific explanation and the technological success of modern science (see Minsky's comment below, for example). On the contrary, of course, determinism is a theological doctrine and the problem is a behavioral problem, and both of these antedate modern science and its explanations and its technological successes: If God created the world and saw to it all, right down to the fall of every Zilch particle, then the real world and all its goings-on are simply a technological exercise reflecting his competence (omnipotence), but in that case how can we, who are merely Elements in that exercise, have any real authorship, responsibility, or freedom in connection with it, since everything that happens happens as a matter of necessity and could not be otherwise?

Just as the C-E formula is a truncated version of a Means-Ends representation, the secular doctrine of "determinism" is the correspondingly truncated version of the theological doctrine. Just as we have the experimenter manipulating the independent variables, from which the rest follows, so we have God manipulating the independent variables from which the history of the world follows. And just as we may refuse to recognize the experimenter in giving our theoretical accounts of his works, so in our secular doctrine, we may refuse to give any cognizance to God in giving our ideological account of all that clockwork. Historically, the truncation was symbolized by the celebrated comment that "We have no need for that hypothesis" (the hypothesis of God as the author). Instead of explaining the nonaccidental character of what actually happens by saying that it was *seen* to, we say, as a matter of ideological principle, that the long sequence of C's and E's (the causal version of the Event version of LC-I) just *happens* to be *necessary*.

The advantages of the move from the theological doctrine to its secular version appear to be entirely emotional and political rather than more generally intellectual or scientific, since the behavioral problem remains the same. (Actually, it is worse in the secular version, for the theological version allowed a solution of sorts.) Briefly, the behavioral problem is that all our behavior has the status of E in the C-E formula and we become redundant "middle terms" in a causal chain. If X causes B and B causes Y, then X causes Y and B drops out of the formula as redundant. As members of a causal chain we have neither any choice about what behavior we engage in nor, correspondingly, any responsibility for our behavior or its consequences. This conclusion violates what we take to be essential features of our behavior generally and it denies those features which we are legitimately at least as certain about as we can be about any scientific account, hence it raises questions about the substantive adequacy of scientific accounts of behavior. Among the behavioral characteristics which are denied are characteristics which are presupposed by any scientific behavior, hence the doctrine raises questions about the methodological adequacy of scientific accounts of behavior.

The difficulties posed by "determinism" may be seen as a limiting case of the "sociology of knowledge" dilemma created by the joint consideration, in the traditional manner, of the historical and methodological connections between behavioral science and the real world. For if the accounts we give scientifically are merely the (causal) product of our personal-social histories, then they are at least parochial if not completely off the mark; but then how could such accounts rise to the level of generality and objectivity required of scientific accounts? Yet the substantive burden of our scientific accounts of behavior is that all our behavior, including our scientific behavior, is just such a causal product. Indeed, our ideologically committed theorists have, as a group, not hesitated to use historical accounts as flanking attacks on the methodological or substantive opposition. Thus, for example, Minsky (1965) comments as follows:

> If one thoroughly understands a machine or a program one finds no urge to attribute *volition* to it. [There is, however, a tendency to resist the reduction of volition to mechanistic principles that] has its genesis in a strong defense mechanism. Briefly,

in childhood we learn to recognize various forms of aggression and compulsion, and to dislike them, whether we submit or resist. Older, when told that our behavior is controlled by such and such set of laws we resist this compulsion as we would any other. Although resistance is logically futile the resentment persists and is rationalized by defective explanations, since the alternative is emotionally unacceptable.

That such a treatment of volition and mechanism could appear in a scientific journal some fifteen years after the major works of Ryle, Austin, Wisdom, and Wittgenstein and be cited with evident approval five years later in a "theoretical" psychological journal hardly needs commentary. So long as the historical aspects of science are isolated from its methodological and substantive aspects in the way they have been, causal-historical appeals will continue to provide disguised ad hominem arguments in the service of deterministic scientific ideologies. But appeals to history in this way undermine *all* scientific theorizing and methodology, and it is characteristic of such rhetoric as Minsky's that there is always a counterrhetoric. Thus, for example, Gil might comment to Wil as follows:

> If one thoroughly understands a human being one finds no urge to consider his behavior as simply the operation of machinery. There is, however, a tendency to insist on the reduction of behavior to mechanistic principles that has its genesis in a strong defense mechanism. Briefly, in childhood we learn the reality principle that we cannot have everything we want, but we dislike and resent it. Older, we are told that our rational behavior is limited not merely by what we are capable of doing in a brute way, but also by our limited outlook, by the rights of others, by the choices which are actually open to us, and by our accountability to ourselves and others for those choices. But we resent and resist these limitations as we did the others. Although resistance is logically futile, since we cannot voluntarily abrogate our responsibility for our behavior, the resentment persists and

is rationalized by defective explanations portraying a nonrational world from which every possible infantile satisfaction might be extorted, since the alternative is emotionally unacceptable.

As we saw initially, the historical aspect of science can easily be developed in such a way that it seems to follow that all our knowledge is idiosyncratic and parochial (because it is merely a causal product of local and temporary sociocultural processes). From such conclusions it would follow that our behavior is poorly informed and our knowledge of behavior is seriously defective, hence we can do little better than to blunder about and muddle along, though of course it doesn't ordinarily seem that way to us. With such limited knowledge, competence, and opportunities, our behavioral choices and the responsibility for making them are correspondingly limited. Determinism provides a limiting case here because any of its nontrivial variants involve the denial of *any* genuine choice or responsibility (in the sense both of authorship of actions and of accountability for them). That denial, however, is enough to make determinism incompatible with our having any knowledge at all, including the knowledge or belief that determinism is the case. (See, e.g., Wick (1964), for a discussion of the tie between freedom and truth.) Since no set of possible observations would amount to having *discovered* that "determinism" is really the case, i.e., since "determinism" is not empirical, though it is presented as a "thesis," we may suspect that the hold it has exercised on our scientific imagination after working hours reflects a confusion between substantive notions and status notions or between facts and doctrines. Let us use a behavioral example in order to gain some further light on the matter.

Consider a game of chess as a paradigm case of human behavior, embodying as it does the notions of freedom, choice of behaviors, and responsibility for those choices, both in terms of authorship and in terms of answerability. Let us suppose two observers, Wil and

Gil, who provide contrasting accounts of that behavior. And let us suppose that Gil, at least, is himself a chessplayer, so that he understands the options that are involved and the nature of the choices that were made.

Gil, on observing Black's tenth move, might say "Yes, he would have to do that" and assemble the relevant considerations (including Black's level of competence) into a compelling case. Wil, who cared only that the move could have been predicted with a scientifically respectable likelihood of success from this set of considerations (or, indeed, any set), might conclude that he had found the decisive constraints, the causal determinants, the controlling variables as it were, of the making of that move, and he would give a C-E account of Black's move.

We, along with Gil, would find Wil's description substantively defective (not false) as an account of that *chess move*. His choosing, from the descriptive options left open by the observable facts, to give *that* description would tell us more about his motives or cognitive limitations than about what went on in the chess game. Of course, Wil might have a reason for *pretending* to know or care only about the predictive relation, and if we knew that, then his choosing to act on *that* reason from among the reasons open to him in those circumstances would tell us primarily about his character or about the nature of the social practice *he* was engaging in (after all, he might be a psychologist). If he were charged with this by Gil, he might agree but then claim that his character was in turn determined by his history so that, true to his lights, *he* had no choice of behaviors. Whereupon Gil would reply that since the historical facts do not force him to give that account of his character, his *choosing* to give *that* account tells us more about his motives and character than about the effects of his history. And so on.

Note that this is not a symmetrical argument. On the surface, it appears that Wil and Gil are involved in a chicken-and-egg type of situation where every thesis meets its counterthesis and there is no resolution but only an infinite progress. This appearance stems from the fact that Wil has presented himself as being a piece of machinery something like a phonograph record whose sound emissions are merely symptoms of some determining prior events, and, like a phonograph record, this is what he keeps repeating.

In a recent attempt to present determinism as an intelligible thesis, Honderich (1970) agrees that determinism is incompatible with personal responsibility. He then considers the question of whether the belief that our behavior and beliefs are physically determined would properly lead us to a general skepticism about the truth of our beliefs. He rejects this conclusion, saying that we would still have *exactly the basis that we do now have* for appraising the truth of our beliefs and that it would be unreasonable to expect determinism to guarantee the truth of our beliefs. He concludes that doubts about our knowledge are not a consequence of determinism and will not provide an argument against determinism.

It does not require exceptional diagnostic acumen to see here a glossing over of the distinction between substantive notions and status notions. On Honderich's defense of determinism, the substance of the beliefs we hold to be true would be no different from what it would be anyhow because, on the determinist view, our procedures for deciding what the facts are would be no different (after all, determinism is not an empirical doctrine). But the determinist thesis, if it has any intelligible content at all, would connect both our beliefs and our checking procedures necessarily to causal antecedents (note that this is at the formula level, not at the level of actual descriptions of causal antecedents). In contrast, it would leave entirely open the connection between our beliefs and our checking procedures and the facts which we take to be the case. But beliefs and checking procedures which had only an unknown relation to the facts could not possibly have the status of *true* beliefs or *valid* checking procedures. No checking procedure of the sort envisioned by the determinist could confer the status of "true," "correct," "verified," "confirmed," "probable," or any other status on a statement or belief. We might, then, just as well adopt a simple coin toss as the basis for adopting, checking, or justifying our beliefs.

So Honderich is quite right in saying that doubts about our knowledge will not provide an argument against determinism. Likewise, doubts about the validity of the beliefs of phonograph records are not grounds for arguing about the existence of phonograph records. This is not, as Honderich appears to suggest, because the existence of phonograph records is compatible with their having true beliefs, but rather because no question about the beliefs of phonograph records can be coherently stated, and so there is nothing of that sort to be doubted, either.

The incoherence of Wil's and Honderich's deterministic stance shows up in the following paradox. Wil has only attempted to present himself as a kind of phonograph record, but he has not succeeded, and this is not just because Gil always has a counterargument. If Wil did succeed in his purported presentation and Gil accepted Wil at face value as a kind of phonograph record, Gil would, of course, be immediately inclined to put *it* in a museum or take it into the laboratory and study it, or perhaps destroy it out of hand as a patent public danger (an "attractive nuisance"—a phonograph record that could easily be mistaken for a human being, with potentially tragic consequences). But the inclination to do any such thing would be only temporary. For if Gil did allow himself to be persuaded by Wil he would have granted that Wil had proclaimed a thesis and successfully presented himself as a kind of phonograph record. But then Gil would have granted Wil a status that no phonograph record of any sort could have or even aspire to. A phonograph record is not *eligible* to present theses or engage in self-presentation. It is no more eligible to do these things or even to try to do them than it is eligible to have beliefs or knowledge. At this point the inclination to lock *it* up would have disappeared and Gil would give Wil an irritated look and continue the conversation if he were so inclined. Thus, Wil could appear to succeed only if he in fact failed to substantiate his deterministic thesis, whereas if he failed it would be an honest failure (phonograph records are not eligible to fail in substantiating theses, either).

In summary, then, the lure of determinism lies in the combination of several things. It promises a guarantee of a certain kind of order in the world, just as the corresponding theological doctrine promised a certain kind of order in the world. It provides a rationalization for an entrenched mode of scientific theorizing. And it provides a liberal supply of polemic material against one's opponents. I have tried to make it easier to see (a) that no such guarantee is possible or required, (b) that cause-effect formulations need no such rationale, and that behavioral science is impossible if restricted to causal accounts, and (c) that "determinism" even when professed only as a matter of scientific faith and not of fact could only be a hairy-chested social posturing and not a possible intellectual position. In short, as with other theological doctrines, so with determinism—in science "we have no need for that hypothesis."

C. "DETERMINISM" FROM A SUBSTANTIVE BEHAVIORAL STANDPOINT

What we have just completed is an exercise in keeping track of historical, substantive, and methodological aspects of scientific statements in order to stay clear of certain temptations and dilemmas. In Section I it was suggested that to suppose that in behavioral science methodology and theory can be kept in separate domains is, on the face of it, preposterous. The problem of "determinism" gives a particular point to that remark.

Nevertheless, the preceding presentation was primarily in the methodological style that is a familiar feature of our customary ways of dealing with those problems which we customarily identify as "methodological." As such it is not very different from a common piece of philosophical writing and has many of the same drawbacks. In this section I propose to deal with the problem of determinism by making explicit use of some behavioral science concepts in a substantive way. The point of the exercise is, first, to show that it can be done at all and, second, to show a gain in perspicuity, economy, and definitiveness when the problem is approached in this way.

The substantive framework for this exercise is provided by Garfinkel's analysis of the successful status degradation ceremony, which was presented in discursive and systematic forms in Section III. To review the necessary conditions:

1). There is a community of individuals who share certain basic values such that adherence to those values is a condition for retaining good standing in the community, i.e., for being fully and simply "one of us."

2). In principle, three members of the community are involved, i.e., a Perpetrator, a Denouncer, and (some number of) Witnesses.

3). The Denouncer and the Witness act as members of the community and as representatives of the community. That is, their behavior reflects their good standing in the community, and they act in the interest of the community rather than out of merely personal interest.

4). The Denouncer describes the Perpetrator as having committed a certain Act.

5). The Denouncer redescribes the Act (if necessary) in such a way that its incompatibility with the community's values follows logically.

6). The Denouncer presents (implicitly or explicitly) a successful case for judging that the Perpetrator's engaging in the Act as redescribed is a genuine expression of his character and is not to be explained away by reference to chance, accident, coincidence, atypical states, etc.

Under these conditions the ceremony is successful, for the Denouncer has shown that the Perpetrator isn't now, and never really was, "one of us." ("What he is now is what, 'after all', he was all along.") The significance of the degradation is that it constitutes a change of status for the Perpetrator, and the significance of that change is that it constitutes a restriction in his eligibilities to participate in certain ways (as certain Elements) in the social life of the group. The limiting case is a total restriction, hence death or expulsion from the group.

Let us now consider the presentation of a deterministic thesis as an attempted degradation ceremony, in order to ask then whether such an attempt could be successful. First, we shall want to ask, Within what value community is such a thesis presented? Since the thesis is presented as one which is true (or at least, as one which ought to be believed), and as a truth which it is important to know, the answer would be, a community of individuals who are characterized as follows:

(a) They are capable of distinguishing between truth and untruth.

(b) They value truth over untruth.

(c) They are capable of choosing to act on beliefs legitimately regarded as true and refusing to act on beliefs contrary to these.

132

(d) They value acting on true beliefs over acting on false beliefs.

(e) They hold each other accountable for so acting.

It would appear that all of the political communities of which we have a historical record have subscribed to these values. However, these values are not as salient a feature in political ideology generally as they are in the ideology of "the academic world," and currently it is primarily within this context that deterministic theses are presented.

Next, we may ask, Who are the Elements in this attempted degradation ceremony? Clearly, the determinist is the Denouncer and all of us are Witnesses. But now an element of strangeness creeps in, for all of us are Perpetrators also. This follows from the nature of the denunciation.

What the determinist tells us is that every one of our behaviors individually and all of them collectively qualify as the Act. "Take any of your day-to-day behaviors," he says. "You took it that you chose that behavior on the basis of at least some valid reasons and true beliefs about yourself and the world and that you were responsible for that behavior. But in fact your choice was an illusion because all of your behavior is antecedently determined by unknown causes. Since it is, and you make no choices, you are not responsible for it, either. And since your beliefs are also antecedently determined, your belief that you can distinguish what is so from what isn't so is also an illusion. And, of course, all of this applies to all of us, including me, and all the time, including now."

In short, the determinist tells us that all our behaviors violate conditions (a) and (c), above, and consequently violate (b), (d), and (e) also. Further, he assures us that this violation is not to be excused or explained away at all, but is, rather, a necessary and essential feature of us and our behavior.

Thus, we have achieved here the spectacle of an individual who acts *as* a member of a responsible, truth-knowledgeable, behavior-choosing community, addresses himself *to* other such members, and says that no one qualifies as a member of such a community. When you come right down to it, says the determinist, *none of us is really one of us!*

Or ever really was at all. I take it that this formulation shows in the clearest possible way what is wrong with determinism in any of its methodologically significant forms. What is wrong is not that it is false, nor yet that it is true. It could not be either of these, for it does not get beyond simply being ridiculous.

Note that although the deterministic "thesis" is the fraternal twin of the religious "We are all of us sinners! Repent and bear witness!" the latter does not fail in the same way. A sinner does lose some status, but he is eligible to repent and bear witness. In contrast, a mechanism neither has nor could have any rights, obligations, or human eligibilities. It is not eligible to bear witness to its being a mechanism, or to regret it, or to discuss the possible truth of the statement that it is a mechanism, or to advise other mechanisms that they *are* mechanisms, or to explain that it didn't really mean *literally* mechanisms, et cetera. This is why the conversation between Gil and Wil could only *be* a conversation so long as Wil failed to carry his "point."

I commented in the earlier, "methodological" formulation that the critical move was to identify the change-of-status significance of the deterministic thesis and not to confuse it with a substantive, or merely factual, significance which could always be hypothesized away by the thesis. I dealt there with the truth status of our beliefs and with the change in that status which the thesis implied. The contribution of the degradation ceremony analysis in this respect is twofold. First, it deals explicitly, but in a formal (content-free) way, with a kind of change-of-status situation, hence it brings the critical feature of the situation out into the open. One might say, following Wittgenstein, that it transforms latent nonsense into patent nonsense. Secondly, it is able to do this because it provides a moderately rich representation of a set of related statuses (Denouncer, Perpetrator, etc.). Because of these relationships and the unity of the larger structure (given by a Configuration description of the degradation ceremony) in which each status has a place, these status concepts are substantially complex and capable of embodying some relatively refined and precisely delineated distinctions. (Compare "True" and "Denouncer" in regard to complexity and conceptual content.) The construction of such representations of complex behavioral processes is part of the substantive work of behavioral science. That such behavioral concepts provide a more sophisticated and economical analysis of a methodological issue than an overtly methodological approach in this case is neither exceptional nor accidental; for, as indicated earlier, methodological facts are behavioral facts, and a scientific codification of behavioral facts ought to be helpful in keeping those facts straight without indulging in paradox.

No doubt the unfamiliarity of the degradation ceremony as an explicitly codified social process has made the latter approach to determinism appear to be more complex and effortful than is actually necessary. Likewise, the unfamiliarity of the general procedure of dealing with methodological issues in a substantively behavioral way contributes to the same result. However, this lack of familiarity is a historical accident and the present difficulty of such an approach is a reality constraint which could be expected to diminish over time. One can readily imagine a state of affairs in which behavioral scientists would routinely master a variety of paradigmatic social process representations in much the same way that a logician or mathematician now routinely masters a variety of argument forms. Currently, a logician, on encountering a particular argument for the first time may readily shrug it off with the comment "fallacy of affirming the consequent." His mastery of this (behavioral) pattern of argumentation gives him the conceptual and technical resources for doing this legitimately. Similarly, our imaginary scientist, on being faced with "determinism" for the first time would have the conceptual and technical resources to shrug it off with the comment "unsuccessful degradation ceremony."

A final comment is in order here before we proceed to the problems of self and self-concept. With determinism, as with reductionism and atomism, no single, definitive argument is to be expected. In general, argumentation generates opposition or reflects preexisting opposition and so agreement is not often or easily arrived at. One can always introduce a new variation or demand to be shown, ad infinitum, how it could apply to other particulars. One can always strike a lofty pose and complain languidly that, really, it just wasn't made clear *enough* to pass one's critical standards. And one can always engage in some variant of Minsky's degradation formula as an excuse for not dealing with the argument at all, e.g., "That's just one man's opinion—where does he get off talking as though he had a pipeline to the Truth?" (The latter is a common sort of reaction to presentations of portions of the Person Concept in spite of explicit and repeated reminders that the presentation and the concept are not eligible for truth values at all.)

Thus, another reminder: The point of the foregoing presentation is not to provide a definitive argument to the effect that "determinism" is, scientifically, neither necessary nor desirable, possible, or intelligible. Rather, it is an illustration of how the substantive representation of the real world or portions thereof (in this case, a human social process) can be used economically and effectively in dealing with a methodological issue. For this purpose the illustrative presentation needs only to provide a nontrivial degree of economy and effectiveness, though to be sure, the more the better.

As in the case of the symmetries between the atomistic and holistic formulations, the behavioral "None of us is really one of us!" formulation shows what is wrong with determinism as a purported thesis without asserting that it is defective in this or that particular way. Anyone who understands that formulation in its behavioral context will have got the point of keeping track of substantive and methodological status aspects of statements so as to identify cases where issues of status (e.g., being "one of us") are passed off as merely factual issues. And so he will not be easily imposed upon by any amount of ingenuity exercised along the lines of "But may it not be the case that, no matter what we think, *actually* . . . ?" We have already had it told centuries ago that the ways of God are mysterious to man, and we have lived through the charm of Descartes' demon who systematically deceives us, and there is no return to theological innocence. Actually, as I have indicated, the rhetoric is more often along the lines of "But *must* it not be the case that, no matter how it seems to us, *actually*, . . . , because modern science requires it, and after all, *it works*, doesn't it?" Innocence comes in many forms. It is not always an asset in behavioral science.

D. SELVES WITHOUT PARADOX:
    A "Methodological" Exercise

In the preceding section we saw how a substantive behavioral formulation can be used to deal economically and effectively with an issue which was traditionally considered to be a purely methodological issue or, even, a philosophical one. We turn now to a substantive problem in order to illustrate how a "methodological" perspective can make a "substantive" contribution. Both the present demonstration and the previous one are intended to give some substance to the general suggestion made at the outset, i.e., that the logical separation of theory and methodology, far from being necessary in behavioral science, is paradoxical and self-defeating.

The phenomenon which provides our substantive problem is that of self-knowledge. A person knows about himself as a person, and his doing so is one of his essential characteristics as a person. A special case of this phenomenon is that scientists, who are necessarily persons, know (or wonder) about what they do *as* scientists, and this kind of self-knowledge is the locus of "methodological" issues and principles.

It is because the domain of methodology is a part of the domain of self-knowledge and one which has been extensively studied in its own right that a "methodological" perspective can contribute substantively to our understanding of the wider domain of self-knowledge.

However, there is a second connection which is essential here. The domain of methodology is the domain of methodological statuses, and that is a part of the more extensive domain of status in general. It is the more general notion of status which we shall need in dealing with the phenomenon of self-knowledge.

As a preliminary move, therefore, let us briefly review and examine the relation between "methodological" and "status."

Initially, reference was made to the methodological, substantive, and historical connections between science and the real world. There, the contrast was drawn between the substantive (theoretical or descriptive) content of a description and the methodological status of that description. The latter notion was elaborated by reference to the putative value of the description (reflecting its derivation) and hence its standing (status) within the historical community and social institution in which it had a use and a value. (Note that this one consideration involves substantive, methodological, and historical features in a logically interrelated and non-paradoxical fashion.)

The second major reference was to the "methodologically oriented" Person Concept as contrasted with the "pictorially oriented" theories of traditional physical and biological sciences and their behavioral counterparts. A major part of this contrast had to do with the contrast between "reality" as a content-free methodological concept and "the real world" as a content-free substantive concept (substantive, because it will include the concept of something which would be simply and literally portrayable, hence the "naturalistic" character of the "natural sciences").

Finally, in connection with the degradation ceremony, the notion of status entered in again in the statement that the success of a successful degradation ceremony consisted in the lowering of the status (the degradation) of the Perpetrator within the community.

What we need to see here is that the relevant contrasts which were drawn in terms of methodological status and descriptive, or substantive, content will also hold in regard to the general concept of status. For example, just as one cannot simply discover the status of a statement by examining the statement and understanding what it says, so one cannot "read off" the status of a person simply by inspecting him, no matter how closely. This is so even though there are both linguistic and nonlinguistic conventions for assigning statuses to statements, and similarly for persons. Thus, there is always a distinction to be made between X (e.g., a person or a statement) and the status of X (e.g., "one of us" or "True" or "scientific"). Correspondingly, there is a contrast between (a) the specification or identification of X by means of some form of representation and (b) the status of that specification.

It is this contrast which I referred to initially in distinguishing between the substantive and methodological connections between science and the real world. As we noted in connection with Chronological description in Section III, we cannot tell from examining a statement that it is a description of the real world. The content of the description is distinct from its status as a description of the real world, and the same would hold for the content of an observation and its status as an observation of the real world. (There is a direct parallel in the notation of symbolic logic: In the formula $(\exists x)F(x)$ the content of the statement is given by $F(x)$; the *putative* status of the statement as a description of the real world is given by the "existential operator" $(\exists x)$.)

In the light of the earlier development in Sections II, III, and V, it should be clear that an essential feature of both methodological status and the general notion of status is that a part-whole relationship is implied. An X has no status except within a wider context which includes X, and this holds whether X is a person, a statement, a subatomic particle, a logical formula, or whatever. Similarly, the difference between the mere doing of B and the knowledge of the doing of B involves a part-whole relationship in a central way. For there could be no such phenomenon as my knowing that I did B, if the facts of the matter included nothing beyond just those facts which were jointly identical to the fact that I did B.

The condition noted above, i.e., that an X has no status except within a wider context which includes X, becomes apparently problematical and potentially paradoxical when X is a theory whose range of reference is universal (i.e., it "applies to everything") for then it seems that nothing lies outside the scope of the theory, hence the notion of there being a wider context appears questionable. This is commonly supposed to be the case, e.g., with regard to the "universal" theories of physics. The wider context, however, is a larger domain of facts, not a larger set of "referents." Since not all facts are physical facts, there is no difficulty in principle with the notion of a wider context in this and similar cases. As we noted in Section II, an object is not per se a physical object any more than it is an economic, theological, aesthetic, or behavioral, etc., object, hence "universal" applicability is not unique to physics. Nevertheless, because of the pictorial and referential character of traditional scientific theorizing, the additional range of facts which makes it possible for scientific theories to have the status that they do (i.e., for those theories to *be* scientific theories) has been codified, when at all, separately and in a nonscientific way as "methodology" and "philosophy of science."

But "methodological principles" are not merely philosophers' theories concerning some scientifically irrelevant features of the behavior of scientists. Rather, they are designed to formulate what it is that carries weight with scientists *as* scientists, hence also what *ought* to carry weight with those persons who make a living as practitioners of science. In point of fact, the practice of science is *much* more concerned with assigning statuses ("empirically confirmed," "significant at the .05 level," "experimentally demonstrated," "operationalized," etc.) to statements than it is with the substantive content of the statements themselves. It will not matter, therefore, if many scientists engage in such procedures without much self-awareness or critical reflection—it is enough that all could do so. On this basis, therefore, methodological status concepts do belong to the domain of self-knowledge in the special case of scientific self-knowers.

Thus, we return to our point of departure, namely, that a methodological perspective may be expected to be of some value in giving a substantive account of the phenomenon of self-knowledge. Let us, therefore, turn to some of the problems which are found in the scientific use of "self-concept" as a "theoretical construct." The difficulties we have created in our scientific management of this notion have lent an air of paradox to the phenomenon itself.

The traditional scientific treatments of this subject reflect the even more traditional distinction between "the self as knower" and "the self as known." More specifically, the scientific notion of "self-concept" appears to be identical to the older notion of "the self as known." Thus, the self-concept is conceived by self-theorists essentially as the substantive content of a person's description of himself. (The fact that one never does, and very likely couldn't, actually give a description which exhausted one's self-knowledge is not to the point here.)

Since it is conceived in this way, certain observable facts, including some experimental findings, become notably intractable from a theoretical standpoint.

For example, it has often been noted that human beings are remarkably resistant to changing their self-concepts in a negative direction in the face of substantially negative information about themselves even when that negative information is veridical and admittedly so.

If a person's self-concept is taken to be simply a summary of the facts he knows about himself, then this resistance to change looks for all the world like peculiar, and defective, information processing. Accordingly, our theoretical explanations have taken the form of introducing a universal, built-in motivation, need, or system principle which has the effect of biasing a person in the direction of a favorable self-description at the cost of distorting the facts. Thus, we have such notions as "protecting" the self-concept (or self-system or self-esteem) or of ego *defenses*, etc. Correspondingly, we have such scarcely disguised hortatory concepts as "being open to experience," "symbolizing one's experience," "having access to one's experience," "reality principle," "ability to tolerate one's unconscious," and so on.

The theoretical move to a built-in bias toward a favorable self-description at the cost of distorting reality is apparently inevitable, given the relevant observational facts. Such a move has the fundamental disadvantage that it implies that people are basically irrational (a degradation ceremony again, and a variation of the determinism paradigm). Consequently, the theory itself becomes suspect, as does all of our theorizing, and then so does the biasing principle, and the net result is a substantive and methodological zero.

For example, since the coherent use of such a theory or principle presupposes that the user of the theory has the veridical account of the matter (for how else could he know that the subject of his description was distorting the facts?), the use of the theory accomplishes a favorable self-description for the user (he, at least, is not distorting the facts here). The phenomenon is well known. The psychoanalyst is always one-up on the patient because he can dismiss any disagreement with "You're (he's) only saying that because you're (he's) repressing (rationalizing, projecting, etc.)" Likewise, the know-nothing behaviorist is always one-up because he can dismiss disagreement with "You're only saying that because of your history of reinforcement and the controlling variables in your environment right now." (See Minsky, above.) And the know-nothing methodologist can dismiss anything whatever by saying "You're only saying that because you're stuck with your arbitrary system of concepts and principles." But the victim of such gamesmanship inevitably learns to turn it upon the manipulator by suggesting that he himself was achieving a favorable self-description at the cost of distorting facts. ("No, *you're* the one who . . . !") Or he may engage in a private degradation ceremony ("Psychologists —yech!"), as a substantial segment of our society has done.

And it will not help matters any to restrict the principle formally to cases which are "ego-involving," along with the implication that persons who are not ego-involved in the matter at hand will be able, without paradox, to detect the bias in the judgments of persons who are so involved. Such a view was, almost certainly, part of the traditional methodological (metamethodological?) view that the ideal of the scientist is to be the neutral, dispassionate, uninvolved observer. However, all this does is to provide a more

143

specific formulation of the reflexive argument—"All that shows is how ego-involved you are in not being ego-involved; as it happens, *I* have no such hang up. . . ."

The long and short of it is that the appeal to irrationality as a "naturalistic" principle of human behavior initially appeared, from a substantive standpoint, to be the Archimedean fulcrum which would give us a world of leverage on "mental" phenomena; it has turned out instead to be the self-contradiction which turns the whole notion of explanation and understanding into methodological nonsense.

Ironically, there has recently come into scientific prominence the long-familiar fact that a number of persons have a negative self-concept which is remarkably resistant to positive information about themselves, even when that information is admittedly positive and veridical. These are often persons who are clinically depressed or who belong to socially oppressed minorities. Thus, any simple notion that people are just irrationally well-disposed toward themselves is directly untenable, and theoretical "explanations" have become correspondingly involuted, ad hoc, and more obviously unsatisfactory. We are left not with explanations but with restatements, in various theoretical idioms, of the fact that a person's self-concept has a mysterious inertia relative to informational influences.

What does not seem particularly mysterious is why traditional scientific theories should be in such difficulties concerning the phenomenon of self-knowledge. For if scientific methodology gets at the facts of self-knowledge insofar as that is scientifically relevant, and if methodological theorizing is not only substantively non-overlapping in relation to scientific theories but also has a logically distinct form, i.e., noncausal, then it would hardly seem surprising that scientific theorizing as we have known it is, in effect, designed to ignore or deny the phenomenon of self-knowledge rather than to elucidate it.

From the nature of the earlier development in this paper and in this section, it would seem that the most obviously weak link in the traditional explanations is the initial presupposition that the self-concept is an information summary. As soon as we distinguish status from content we have available a noninformational component in the situation, so that if the self-concept is not simply responsive to information, then the obvious move is to codify that sort of fact by assimilating the self-concept essentially to what is noninformational in the general behavioral situation and only secondarily to what is informational.

For example, one way to deal with the phenomenon of self-knowledge is to consider person's self-concept to be not a factual summary of his information about himself, but rather his summary formulation of his status. In order to pursue this approach, however, we shall require some further preliminary work.

So far, our analysis of the degradation ceremony has provided us with a representation of a certain kind of status change, namely, status reduction. I have spoken, however, of status assignments generally, and not merely of status reductions. Clearly, we need a symmetrical formulation embodying positive status change. It takes little imagination to conceive of a ceremony which would resemble the degradation ceremony in its general form but would differ in just those ways which would qualify it as an "accreditation ceremony." (In his presentation of the degradation ceremony, Garfinkel comments, "Structurally, a degradation ceremony bears close resemblance to ceremonies of investiture and elevation.") Methodologically, the difference between accreditation and degradation is a difference in detail. Having gone this far, we may now imagine a more complex form of ceremony in which elements of accreditation and degradation may be present in any proportion. It is this more complex, or more noncommittal, notion which is involved in "assigning a status."

And there may be a point in the reminder that status assignments need not involve any ceremonial behavior. Just as we normally do simple sums "in our heads" rather than "out loud," so we commonly make status assignments in our heads rather than out loud. In both cases the observable ceremony serves as a paradigm for *what* it was that got done "in our heads." The mark of our having made a status assignment is that we behave toward X in accordance with the status we assign to X.

The preceding sentence will have to be read in a certain way. It is not that the different sorts of behavior are primarily important as evidence that a status assignment has taken place, but as mere *evidence* are (a) inferior to the observation of an *actual* status assignment ceremony, and (b) never *conclusive* evidence of the occurrence of the hypothetical "inner" or "mental" status assignment whose occurrence is therefore always problematical. Rather, it is the distinction between the different sorts of behaviors that is the whole point in talking about status assignments to begin with. Without that kind of follow-through, an overt ceremony would be merely an idle gesture, a case of going through some motions; conversely, given such a follow-through, anyone who utters such words as "But was the status assignment really made?" has the burden of showing that there is any such question to be asked. (For one can also say "But was a question about status assignment really asked?")

What, then, if not information, is involved in status and the assignment of status? We noted earlier that status goes with *eligibility* to participate in the practices of a community in certain ways. The correlative of this is what we have just noted above, i.e., that an individual's eligibility to participate in certain ways in certain practices can be formulated from the standpoint of other participants in the same practices. When we do that, we arrive at the notion of *their* treating him in certain ways (treating him as an X). We have also noted that status implies a part-whole relation-

146

ship, i.e., embeddedness in a wider context, and that the wider context is not per se a more extensive set of referents but rather a wider range of facts (the former is a special case of the latter). We may now elaborate this latter notion and connect it to the notion of "eligibility" by referring to that portion of Section II dealing with "ultimate objects." I said there that ultimate objects must be specified as to kind (cf. Rule 9) and that since kinds of objects are distinguished from one another by the kinds of relationships they can (logically) enter into, the specification of ultimate objects sets limits to the totality of such relationships, hence to the totality of possible states of affairs involving such objects, and hence it defines a kind of "world" in the sense of LC-I. The eligibilities of a human being to participate in a human community is the behavioral form of the same principle. A person's status and eligibilities summarize his relationships with other individuals or groups, and so they set limits to the possible facts concerning him, hence they define a kind of world, i.e., *his* world. In effect, a person is, for himself, an "ultimate object." (We reached something very close to this in Section III where, in briefly generating the theory of empiricism, we noted that for a given observer the real world is the one which includes him *as* an observer.) Finally, it should be clear that status assignments and specifications of ultimate objects are not a matter of "legislating facts" or "making it all up." That is, they are not contra-empirical and do not contrast with *"finding out how the world is."* Rather, to speak of status assignments and ultimate objects is to make explicit the range of possibilities which *would* qualify as facts; it is to make explicit what an observer is capable of finding out in principle. For example, no observation whatever would for us count as having discovered empirically that the table smiled or that it is less than 17. The range of possible facts does not change as a result of observation which determines merely which of those possible facts are the case.

147

From these considerations one might readily draw the conclusion that self-concepts are absolutely impervious to facts. For if one's self-concept is a summary formulation of one's status and if status assignments are a matter of formulating possible facts rather than facts, and if the range of possible facts does not change as a result of observing facts, then it would seem that one's self-concept could not be influenced by one's observations. Thus, we would have a simple (given the prior development) account of the findings noted above, i.e., that a person's self-concept is resistant to change in either the positive or negative direction. Briefly, we would say that a person does not change his self-concept in the face of contrary facts simply because there are no contrary facts—except for some other observer.

For example, just as a socially prejudiced person may quite honestly say "Some of them are extremely talented and intelligent" without for a moment doubting that all of them are really *inferior persons*, so could I, if I had assigned myself the status of "inferior," recognize that I was extremely talented and intelligent without for a moment calling my essential inferiority into question. I would have made some possibly surprising empirical discoveries about what an inferior person is capable of accomplishing. What I would not have done is discovered that I was not inferior since, for any given accomplishment, "When I do it, that's different." Note that in connection with common social statuses and relationships we do not find this phenomenon either surprising or problematical. For example, when the mayor takes a bribe, that is one thing; when a businessman takes a bribe, that's different. The one is a betrayal of public trust; but nothing that the businessman does could be a betrayal of a public trust because he has no such trust to betray— he has no such status.

However, although such an account of self-knowledge would indeed account for the fact that one's self-concept is resistant to change, it so far encounters the opposite problem, namely, that it fails to account for the fact that one's self-concept (a) is initially acquired and (b) does sometimes change. What we may claim so far is to have a coherent account of the fact that one's self-concept is not *simply* responsive to facts, namely, because one's self-concept is not *primarily* or *essentially* a summary of facts. We would have arrived at a formally adequate account if, for example, we were able to say further that although one's self-concept can change as a result of observation, the change itself is a function of one's self-concept, and this is why one doesn't change one's self-concept very readily, and when one does, it is not by discovering that one is really someone else.

In this connection we are reminded that statuses are given and received, and not simply discovered. One's status in the community (or other wider context) cannot be simply self-assigned any more than the status of a description can be simply self-assigned. The status that is given (or offered) to a person by the community is in general the one which is easiest (i.e., most readily implementable, though possibly unpleasant) to act on, and what is refused by the community is in general difficult or impossible to act on. Thus, the discovery that one has been assigned a particular status goes hand in hand, statistically, with the acceptance, or self-assignment, of that status. This is particularly likely if such acceptance requires no change, e.g., if one had been acting in accordance with that status prior to the discovery of the status assignment. (Compare the classic developmental notions of "the generalized other," "the looking-glass self," "the introjected parent," etc.)

Conversely, we might emphasize that although a status which is received may be the easiest one to accept, it must *be* accepted or the status assignment will be more or less of an idle ceremony. To use the classic example, a master-slave relationship cannot be carried off if the designated slave refuses (successfully) to be one.

In this way we are led back to a recognition of an overlooked fact, namely, that human beings generally, and not just scientists, spend a great deal of their efforts on the assignment of statuses rather than on anything simply factual. Much of human, and not merely scientific, interaction can be understood adequately as maintaining particular statuses or as presenting, rejecting, or adjudicating claims to particular statuses. (Compare Erving Goffman's work on self-presentation and Eric Berne's delineation of "games people play.") And in that case we may suspect that the deficiencies of our scientific theories as theories of scientific behavior will be equally prominent when they are appraised as theories of behavior generally.

So far, we have capitalized on the simple introduction of the content-free notion of status in clarifying, systematizing, and integrating some of the phenomena of self-knowledge and the behaviors which "express" or "reflect" such self-knowledge. Let us now consider two elaborations on this simple introduction in order to deal with some further problems raised by the traditional dichotomy of "the knower" and "the known" and with the problem of change of self-concept.

To begin with, consider that although statuses must be assigned and accepted rather than being merely discovered, once a given status has been assigned and accepted (self-assigned) the possession of that status becomes a fact which may be discovered by some observer, including the person in question. (Compare: The making of a promise is a matter of *making* it, and not of *discovering* that one has made it; on the other hand, once it is made, *that* it has been made is a discoverable fact.)

Then consider that for a person to know a fact about himself requires the assignment of a particular *status*, i.e., "factual," to the description or representation of that fact, even when the latter involves the assignment or possession of a particular status.

1. I take it that the fact that in calling a judgment or description "factual" one is making a *"value* judgment" is sufficiently well known and well accepted not to need elaboration here.

2. We encountered this relationship earlier in Section II. There, I said that the methodologically oriented formulation of reality as the boundary condition on our possible behaviors (note, in the light of the present discussion, that this is a status-eligibility formulation and that it reflects the correlative relation between real world and self) could not be replaced by a pictorially oriented *description* of what the constraints on our possible behaviors are, since we would then have to ask how we could act on *that* description, and that amounts to asking what the status of that description would be.

Thus, there is a logical interplay between (a) status assignments, which, as behaviors or achievements, are nonfactual or content-free, and (b) descriptions, which are factual and have content. The most obvious features of this interplay are of the "chicken and egg" variety. However, that familiar paradigm will not do justice to the situation here. The interplay is not between two logically distinct categories having only an external, historical connection. It is, rather, between a particular kind of status, i.e., "factual" ("descriptive," "substantive," "theoretical," etc.), and either (a) other kinds of status or (b) the more general category of "status."

The logical (not causal, ontological, or epistemological) interplay between status assignment and descriptive content requires that they be conceptually distinct, and that appears to be sufficient to resolve the paradoxes generated within our scientific theories by the traditional distinction between "the knower" and "the known." The paradoxes of this sort stem from the fact that, since the knower (the "pure ego") is by definition different from the known (the "empirical ego") and everything that a person knows about himself is by definition part of the known, the question arises how we could possibly conceive of a knower, much less acquire factual knowledge about it (about *what?*). Predictably, our explanatory moves have consisted of accepting one or another of the horns of the dilemma.

The first choice involves a denial that there is a knower that is known (the "no ownership" theory of experience). Since this alternative has been chosen primarily by some philosophers rather than scientists, and since it has not received a definitive exposition, and, finally, since it apparently violates our common observation, I shall not deal with it here. (The ambiguity is such that the present formulation might be taken by philosophers as a "no ownership" view.)

The second choice involves the invention of peculiar sorts of objects to serve as the *real* knower. Thus, for example, self-theorists, such as Carl Rogers, often identify "the organism" (or, it appears, *its* experience) as the real knower, and it (or its experience) is what we (we organisms?) see only darkly through our phenomenological, inferential, and/or symbolic glasses. So we are back to not really having knowledge about ourselves after all. (Unless, perhaps, we are, somehow, "open to experience" or "able to symbolize our experience." That, one would have to suppose, is like being in a state of Grace or undergoing Revelation.)

In contrast, the present formulation in terms of both descriptive content and status assignment shows quite clearly why there is this particular contrast of knower and known. This pair of terms divides precisely along the lines of status and content. "Knower" refers to a particular status (not to some describable characteristic or object) and as such is as content-free as "I," "you," and "($\exists x$)." Small wonder, then, that the existential "I-Thou" relationship has seemed so peculiarly murky and ineffable to a generation of doggedly operationalizing experimenters and "naturalistic" cause-effect theorizers.

Thus, we have arrived at our second elaboration. The assignment of a status was introduced as something which contrasts with discovering facts or giving descriptions. In our first elaboration we saw that the assigning of a status or the possession of a status can be described, post hoc, as a fact, and that to do so is to make a second sort of status assignment, i.e., "factual." Now we see that to describe it as a fact involves or presupposes yet a third sort of status assignment.

For if an individual, P, assigns a status to some X (e.g., to a person or to a description), behaving in this way must be in accordance with P's behavioral possibilities, i.e., it must be in accordance with his status. So "status assigner" is itself a status. Further, "status assigner" implies "knower," since P must distinguish X from Y in order to assign X a different and particular status. And, for example, if Q observes that P assigns a status to S, it follows that both Q and P are status assigners. It is because making a status assignment and acting on it is a case of behavior that one of our traditional dichotomies is the distinction between the "self as *agent*" and the "self as object." When Q and P, above, are the same person, he knows himself not only as a knower, but also as an agent.

(To return for a moment to our Wil and Gil example: It is because a phonograph does not have the status of "status assigner" or "knower" that no sound which emerges from the phonograph is eligible for the status of a statement. Since a phonograph cannot assign its sounds the status of a statement, it can make sounds but it cannot make a statement. Since it is not a status assigner, it could not even assign the status of "mere phonograph" or "non-status-assigner" to itself, and this would be so even if its visible appearance and internal structure were indistinguishable from that of a "determinist." This is why Wil could continue the argument only so long as he failed to make his point. Conversations are between status assigners, and between status assigners it is "I and Thou.")

"Knower" is not, of course, the only second-order status (i.e., one which implies the making of status assignments by that individual). The assignment of a status has no truth value, but since making it and acting on it is a form of behavior, a given assignment by a given person might, as is the case with any behavior, be injudicious, infelicitous, foolish, pointless, etc. Or it might be exceptionally acute, discerning, fortunate, et cetera.

Thus, a person who assigns a status, including the status of "factual," is eligible for criticism on that score by either himself or his status-assigning peers. That criticism will typically take the form of degradation or accreditation, i.e., it will be a status assignment ("pointless," "discerning," and so on). To characterize an experiment as "rigorous," a presentation as "philosophical," or a person as "foolish" is to engage in just such critical, status-assigning behavior. (Note that, indeed, when a foolish person does it, that's different.) Of course, this status-assigning behavior may itself be criticized, and so on. In this way do we evolve the interminable rhetoric of methodological and philosophical "issues" or "positions" within the social institutions of science and philosophy. In this way also does a person's self-concept evolve as a logically complex summary of his factual and critical judgments about his factual and critical judgments and his behavior thereon.

Thus, self-concepts do change, and although factual description enters the picture, such changes begin and end with non-"factual" status assignments. We therefore retain our original account of a person's self-concept as a summary of his status. The relation between this summary and any simply observable facts about him is as indirect as the relation between a scientific theory and its observational "basis," and it is of a similar sort, i.e.,

154

it is his conceptualization of the world which includes both himself as an observer and the facts he observes.

In the traditional theories concerning the self-concept, the phenomenon involves a variety of intractable paradoxes, or else glaring omissions relative to the phenomenon. In the present formulation the phenomenon of self-knowledge appears tractable and systematically comprehensible, though complex. I take the preceding presentation, therefore, to be an illustration of the value and possibility of employing "methodological" concepts in dealing with a "substantive" problem.

Conversely, the formulation of scientific methodology as a limited version of the general phenomenon of self-knowledge also contributes to our understanding of the former. If acknowledging particular facts about himself does not typically lead a person to have a different concept of himself (i.e., assign a new status), it should not be surprising that acknowledging particular negative findings does not typically lead us as scientists to change our theories (i.e., assign them a new truth status). Correspondingly, if our "methodological" theorists have been unable to give an adequate account of the sense in which scientific theories are empirical, it is not surprising that our "scientific" theories have been unable to provide an adequate account of the sense in which a person's knowledge of himself is not empirical.

VI

BEHAVIORAL FACTS
AND BEHAVIORAL SCIENCE

I SUGGESTED INITIALLY that the substantive, methodological, and historical connections between science and the real world would have to be formulated within a behavioral science if there were to be anything which qualified as a behavioral science at all. In the subsequent presentation we have seen the following contributions toward that end.

1. The calculational system involving the reality concepts exhibits these concepts as fundamentally rational, because they are defined systematically rather than referentially, hence scientifically usable in a way that is not possible under the existing ad hoc metaphysical treatment (or presupposition) of these concepts by scientists and their philosophical preceptors. The Reality System, being calculational rather than merely nominative, makes it relatively easy, perhaps even painless, to eschew the traditional reification of biological and physical concepts in the behavioral sciences and to recognize instead that there are different "worlds," or domains of facts. In this connection, it provides a reminder of the fundamental way in which "the real world" is a human invention and a personal and social achievement no less than it is a social norm and that it is not something which is simply, transcendentally, "out there" waiting to be discovered empirically. Part of the force of this re-

156

minder is that, whatever else they may be, facts about the world are behavioral facts because they are facts only for persons and because they have some behavioral significance.

2. The descriptive formats presented in Section III provide us with technical means for delineating real-world phenomena, including behavioral phenomena, in a precise and systematic way. Thus, collectively, they provide us with the notational resources for giving the explicit and detailed representations of behavioral regularities and behavioral patterns which would form the working hypotheses and substantive achievements of a behavioral science. Since observational, hypothetical, and theoretical regularities and patterns are dealt with within the same notational and conceptual framework, the existing problems of differentiating them and then linking them together again do not arise. Thus we need not struggle with the stratification of scientific language into "theoretical" and "observational" vocabularies, or with the reification of "hypothetical constructs" as against "intervening variables." And we can dispense with our Ptolemaic accounts concerning "operationalizing" theoretical concepts, "confirming theoretical hypotheses," purifying our "observation language," and so forth. No doubt there are linguistic and technical complexities in the conduct of science, but they need not be these.

3. In the initial discussion of the methodological connection between behavioral science and the real world I suggested that we do not have an adequate account of the empirical nature of the scientific enterprise. In this connection, the brief elaboration of the concept of "Chronological description" in Section III provides us with a pre-empirical basis for empiricism. The latter, in turn, provides the conceptual basis for understanding science as a social institution having an essential empirical aspect. Thus, the methodological connection between science and the real world is at least partially codified by the theory of empiricism, which provides the

basis for the criticism of scientific accounts on empirical grounds. The historical connection is codified *pro forma* in representing behavioral science and other sciences as social institutions. The substantive connection is given in principle by the Reality System itself (the state-of-affairs system), since it provides the logical grounds of the possibility of giving substantive descriptions of "the real world" as well as the primary technical resources for doing so.

4. The "status" treatment of self-concept and the "degradation ceremony" treatment of "determinism" show not only that substantive and methodological topics can be dealt with within a single logical domain, but also that there is a point in doing so. The treatment of determinism shows how substantive formulations of social behavior can provide the essential logical forms for the methodological analysis and criticism of substantive accounts of behavior.

5. A critical account of the atomistic, reductionistic, and causal-deterministic features of the presently constituted social institution of science exhibits these features as *merely* historical rather than essential in any way. These features are dispensable because they are not part of the scientific enterprise but belong, rather, to a super-imposed and characteristically theological ideology. The dispensability of these features is crucial because, although they have been relatively harmless in connection with the more primitive and incomplete "natural" sciences, they are incompatible with the methodological requirements of a behavioral science. One may easily conclude that it is the historical predominance of this atomistic, reductionistic, deterministic ideology which has prevented the emergence of a behavioral science. The methodological requirements for a behavioral science are different from those for a "natural" science not because of some postulated transcendent or "emergent" feature of behavior, but because for a behavioral science the conduct of that science (hence its methodology) lies within the

scope of its subject matter whereas for any other science this will not be the case.

6. I have begun to illustrate a principle which will later gain in explicitness and importance (in the projected third monograph, which will deal with language and science), namely, that discourse concerning fundamentals must have the general character of presenting, reminding, portraying, or evoking rather than of asserting, proving, arguing, demonstrating, or postulating. This is because, as with questions of proof, raising or answering questions of truth requires an existing framework of concepts, conventions, and procedures, and in discourse concerning fundamentals such a framework either does not exist or cannot be taken for granted. I mention this now because, although the notion that substantive and methodological considerations in behavioral science belong to the same conceptual domain (the domain of behavior) is readily grasped, it is not easily assimilated. For example, one of the implications is that in general one cannot take merely a substantive view or merely a methodological view of a given formulation without missing the point. Thus, what is easy to do, and indeed almost inevitably will be done, is to take the present reminder as a traditionally substantive sort of statement and one which is, therefore, to be appraised by reference to the traditionally "immutable" and pre-existing methodological theories. In the latter connection, for example, the critical reader will very likely miss, and perhaps even resent, the absence of any effort at proof, evidence, or compelling argument. Worse, he is likely to take what I have written as being such an effort. A reminder is therefore in order regarding speaker and listener.

Although I take these to be contributions to the fundamentals of a behavioral science they do not add up to a full-fledged delinea-

159

tion of a behavioral science. As I have indicated several times, any presentation based solely on the reality concepts will be seriously incomplete. It remains to provide a systematic formulation of persons, behavior, and language (see Ossorio, 1966a, 1968, 1969a, 1969b, 1973, for earlier efforts) in order to exhibit scientific behavior as a form of social behavior within a historical institution having the substantive and methodological connections with the real world that we have seen. These formulations will be topics for subsequent monographs. Some preliminary remarks can, however, be made at this time concerning the nature of an adequate conceptual structure for behavioral science. These remarks are organized below around the topics of "subject matter," "totalities," "naturalism," and "being informative." In part, the force of these remarks is that (a) a behavioral science needs a descriptive conceptual system to identify its subject matter and provide formal access to it; (b) a conceptual system adequate for this purpose would, at a minimum, be reflexive, naturalistic, and holistic; and (c) one way to arrive at an appreciation of this necessity is via a critical examination of the traditional approaches, which have none of these features.

A. On Subject Matter

The task which defines a behavioral science could hardly be other than to give intellectual coherence to all the facts of behavior, including (but not restricted to) those which must be discovered to be the case and those which are not yet known to be the case. So, for example, a behavioral science would be concerned with empirical facts and not merely with conceptual constructions or definitional facts. And it would not be merely a post facto or ad hoc reconstruction of behavioral facts, but would necessarily have some predictive applicability. On the other hand, it could not be merely a matter of "prediction and control of behavior," since the prediction and control of behavior is merely another example of the (manipulative) behavior of persons.

Since our paradigm cases of behavior are cases of the behavior of persons, the essential subject matter of behavioral science is the behavior of persons, and it is the distinctively human aspects of their behavior which would constitute the distinctive subject matter of a behavioral science.

It is the essential concern with what is distinctively human which distinguishes behavioral science from biology, physiology, physics, and the other such social enterprises. Conversely, one could say, it is the scope of its concern which distinguishes behavioral science from the traditionally humanistic disciplines such as literature, philosophy, music, law, drama, etymology, and others. To say this might be misleading, however. For example, neither literature nor philosophy is formally limited in the range of phenomena which might come under its purview. In general, however, literature has the form of chronology (cf. "Once upon a time...") and is not substantively cumulative, whereas behavioral science is not restricted in this way. Again, philosophy resembles behavioral science in its emphasis on general and systematic formulations. However, in accordance with our cultural traditions, philosophy deals with subject matters of a special sort (ontology, epistemology, metaphysics, logic, etc.) or in a special way which we have been pleased to call "foundational" ("the philosophy of" art, physics, mind, mathematics, science, et cetera). Philosophy is ad hoc and post hoc, and its traditional topics, concepts, norms, methods, and concerns weigh upon it in a most narrowing way. In contrast, a behavioral science would be both empirical and pre-empirical, both post hoc and predictive, and would be concerned with the full range of facts and possible facts concerning persons, their behaviors, aspects, products, theories, et cetera.

The identification of the behavior of persons as the essential concern of behavioral science is best regarded as definitional rather than polemic, though, indeed, even the characterization as "definitional" is a concession to traditional ways of thinking. I should not want to be taken as denying, for example, that the behaviors of Homo sapiens importantly and systematically resemble the behaviors of other organisms. Those facts and our attempts to codify them and exploit them are behavioral facts. However, there is an asymmetry here. It would seem that a discipline which dealt adequately with distinctively human behavior but not at all with the commonalities between Homo sapiens and other species would qualify as a partially successful behavioral science. In contrast, a discipline which dealt successfully with those commonalities but not at all with distinctively human behavior would not qualify as a behavioral science at all. The fact is that we have such disciplines, biology and comparative psychology, and we would hardly want to hold these up as models of a behavioral science.

It is customary for the theorist who confuses the behavior of persons with the behavior of organisms to pride himself on the generality of his account. Thus, one would not be surprised, in an introductory class in psychology or in the opening pages of a textbook, to find that "Psychology is the study of *all* behavior, i.e., the behavior of organisms, and the behavior of human beings (or Homo sapiens) is merely one small part of that, albeit an important part." In such formulations it follows that the fundamental aspects of human behavior consist of what is common to it and other organismic behavior and that what is distinctively human is nonfundamental.

In this connection, consider the following vignette.

Gil: Why stop at the behavior of organisms? After all, chemical molecules, subatomic particles, tornadoes, and other inanimate objects are commonly said to exhibit behaviors and to "do" things. Why isn't the study of behavior the study of what organisms share with all of those?

Wil: But if it was that, the study of behavior would be physics.

Gil: Well, if it were what you said, the study of behavior would be biology.

There is a different outlook possible on the matter of "all behavior." In the traditional approach the primary identification is of a certain kind of object, e.g., a Homo sapiens, and behavior is what (or whatever) *it* "does." This is a predictable consequence of the "pictorial" methodology discussed in Section II. It is possible, however, to make the primary identification that of human behavior and then derive the concept of a certain kind of object, i.e., "person," as what (or whatever) "does" that sort of thing.

From this we generate the following distinctions: (a) A specimen of Homo sapiens is an organism of a particular species; (b) A person is an individual who engages in human behavior; (c) A human being is a person who is also a specimen of Homo sapiens. Thus:

Gil: As a behavioral scientist, I'm interested in *all* behavior, and not merely and not primarily in the behavior of organisms. Further, the crucial case and the paradigm case is the behavior of persons. The behavior of organisms and particles can be formulated as a case of human behavior with something essential missing. In contrast, human behavior cannot be formulated as the behavior of particles or organisms with something nonessential added. For me the study of behavior encompasses the full range of similarities and differences among behaviors. For you it consists of finding the least common denominator.

163

Much of the preceding reflects a certain criterion of adequacy. It is universally accepted, I take it, that a primary criterion of adequacy for a scientific theory or principle is that it should apply universally within the domain which defines its subject matter. For example, a theory of learning which encompassed only some of the known facts of learning per se or only some of the varieties of learning (this case is a special case of the former) would be ipso facto inadequate as a theory *of learning*, though it might do quite well for some other, limited, purpose, e.g., as a theory of rote nonsense-syllable recall by some contemporary Indo-European speakers. It is this criterion which is being appealed to with the talk of "*all* behavior," and it is the fact that it is a criterion which keeps such talk from being merely grandiose in intent.

More important than the question of intent is the question of fact. How could a formulation be recognized as failing or not failing in regard to universality? The question comes with particular force when it is not theories but the descriptive conceptual system constitutive of the subject matter which is in question. A theory merely has to codify what is observed. The descriptive framework has to codify what is possible in its domain. The conceptual framework, to be adequate, must provide a systematic (and not merely ad hoc) representation of the range of facts which are possible and which, therefore, the corresponding theories (theories about the same subject matter) might have to provide an account of. Further, it must do so in a way which is sufficiently perspicuous to serve as an independent check on the substantive adequacy of such theories. That is, it must serve as an explicit basis for making methodological status assignments. (Could we, for example, make a critical appraisal of the substantive adequacy of a particular theory of learning, personality, or motivation if our only access to the facts of learning (or personality or motivation) was via the theory itself?) The condition of perspicuity will not be met, for example, by a formulation which is excessively vague ("All is one"; "Behavior is what organisms do"; "All behavior is a conditioned response") or excessively ad hoc ("Learning is what learning experiments study"; "We'll know what anxiety is when we've found out all there is to find out about it"; "Good science is whatever emerges from the process of natural selection in the history of a given discipline").

At this point two questions arise. The first is, How does one identify a particular behavior? The second is, Does the fact that a theory applies to all behavior, in the sense indicated above, mark that theory as a behavior theory?

In regard to the latter, the answer is, clearly, "Not at all." In this sense, almost all theories, both scientific and nonscientific, apply to all behavior. Theories of physics, chemistry, biology, economics, theology, esthetics, law, ethics, and many others will qualify. That is, one could point to a case of behavior, B, and say "I'm talking about that" and then proceed to give a correct physical, biological, esthetic, legal (etc.) description of something there. Yet, clearly, none of these is behavioral science, nor have we designated them as such. Psychoanalytic theory, general S-R theories of various sorts, existential theories, attribution theory, and cognitive theories apply to all behavior. There is no presumption therefrom that these are behavior theories or that someone who makes reference to "id," "conditioning," "operant," "expectation," "self-actualization," and so forth is saying anything about behavior.

One might appeal to an additional condition to distinguish behavior theories from among those which apply to all behavior. One might say, "But psychoanalysis (S-R theory, attribution theory, etc.) has a demonstrable utility in the prediction and control of behavior, and that, in addition to its applying to all behavior, makes it a scientific behavior theory."

In this connection we may note that by appealing to prediction and control we have moved from science to technology. Chemical

165

theories may be applied to the making of paint or to the adhesion of paint to highway surfaces. We do not on that account identify chemistry as "the science of paint making" or "the science of highway painting," partly because that would be absurd and partly because, though there might be some point in talking that way, chemistry does not encompass all the facts of paint making or highway painting. If, then, talk of "archetypes," "libido," "operant," "stimulus," "cognitive structure," et al. is effectively pressed into the service of persons who seek to predict and "control" the behavior of others, why would we be at all inclined to call such talk *behavioral* theorizing or such efforts "the science *of behavior*"? We may also note that those individuals who in the past have succeeded in predicting and/or controlling other people's behavior have more often employed physical, astrological, chemical, theological, economic, political, ethical, or other such theories than any of the theories which have historically been presented as behavioral theories. So the additional condition also fails to distinguish nonbehavioral theories from those which are traditionally designated as behavioral theories. We might begin to wonder whether that distinction has any application here.

A physicist may see a baseball batter hit a curve ball out of the park and give an account of the matter in terms of masses, vectors, energy conservation, and so forth. In such a case there is a clear sense in which he is talking about a baseball event, but there is also a clear sense in which he is not talking about a baseball event at all, but merely giving an account of an event and a process within the world of physics. One might explicate the former by saying that this baseball event was the locus of application of the physicist's account. And the latter could be explicated by saying that it is not baseball phenomena but rather facts about motions, masses, vectors, momentum, energy, et cetera, that are the subject matter of physical theories.

166

In short, we need to distinguish between the subject matter of a theory and the loci of its applications or possible applications *by persons*. The considerable ambiguity of the phrase "applies to all behavior" has made it easy to confuse the two. What have traditionally been called "behavior theories" have had behavior as a locus of application, and in this respect they do not differ from physical, theological, economic, and other theories or models. Once the distinction between subject matter and locus of application has been made there could be little excuse for supposing that such theories have had or could have behavior as their subject matter. It is not merely a matter of terminology here. That is, it is not merely that such theories do not contain as part of their theoretical content the expressions with which we designate behavior, persons, patterns of behavior, particular behaviors, circumstances, the relation of persons to their behavior and circumstances, et cetera. Occasionally a theory does contain such expressions, but on most occasions this is a misleading circumstance because the theory does not contain the concept in question. For example, a concept of behavior, or of knowledge or expectancy or value, which has a conceptually built-in "deterministic" causal connection to antecedent circumstances, even purely hypothetical antecedents, is not the concept of behavior, but rather a joke or an equivocation which is an imposition on the reader or listener. Likewise a concept of "the number 17" which was the concept of something black weighing twelve pounds would not be the concept of the number 17, but rather a joke or an imposition.

What we have said about the locus of application may also be said, with some required formal changes, about the locus of study. If we were to ask a physicist (biologist, theologian, etc.) "What do you study *as* a physicist?" he might point to an instance of behavior. So might the biologist, theologian, journalist, etc. The pointing serves only to identify where he might look, not what it is that he studies. The latter is given by the questions he might ask and the answers he might give. Thus, the locus of study is not at all the same as the subject matter under study.

I have made several remarks suggesting more or less directly that there does not at present exist a science of behavior. In general these suggestions have stemmed from a critical methodological perspective. Here we may add the substantive perspective. We do not have a behavioral science because we do not have a science which has or could have all behavior as its subject matter. Only in an isolated and fragmentary way do we have disciplines which have *any* human behavior as their subject matter, and with few exceptions (e.g., some aspects of ethnomethodology, existential theories, and interaction theories of the Erving Goffman genre) they are classified as "Humanities."

How could a science have behavior as its subject matter and not merely as a locus of study or application? Here, we are in part back to the first of the two questions raised above, namely, How does one identify a particular behavior? (Note the resources provided in Section III.) In light of the present issue of subject matter, we may extend the question to ask how we could both distinguish among particular behaviors or kinds of behavior and also have a grasp on all possible behaviors including merely possible behaviors which do not occur and are therefore not observed.

Any talk of "all possible behaviors" is apt to strike people as grandiose, quixotic, or naive, if not actually nonsensical. If we thought that the totality of behavioral possibilities was something we could at best crudely approximate by carefully accumulating historical records of what we (any of us; all of us jointly) have taken to be behavioral facts or possibilities, then, indeed, we should have little choice but to regard any talk of systematizing all behavioral possibilities as hopeless or nonsensical. Very likely, too, we would regard the taking of that stand as simply showing the kind of care and modesty that it is incumbent on a genuinely scientific person to exhibit.

But, clearly, a systematic representation of possible behavioral facts cannot be given in a merely historical way even if we employ however ingenious taxonomic devices. That would be as ridiculous as attempting to represent a language by listing the sentences which we take to have been actually uttered by someone at some time or another. How would we know what to count if that were our only access to the language? *What* is it that we would be taking him to have uttered?

Historically, it has been recursive formulations, hence calculi or calculus-like systems, which have provided us with the finite and present means to encompass nonfinite domains of possible facts in a historically noncommittal way. If we have learned our algebra lessons we will recognize that a given representation is a representation of an algebra problem or procedure, and this is independent of whether we take it that anyone has ever posed or been faced with that particular problem or engaged in that procedure. Nor do we approach the matter with the lurking suspicion that what we have called "algebra" may in fact turn out to be really something else, e.g., football. Similar considerations hold for our recognition of sentences. And, of course, that is the way it is and would have to be for the recognition and representation of possible behaviors.

Perhaps it needs to be said that this kind of knowledge is not in principle mysterious, nor does a fundamental reliance on it create any methodological difficulties or beg any substantive questions. To be sure, there are questions one might ask about this kind of knowledge, but one cannot question it in principle. Historically, psychologists have created a "mystery" of this and many other matters by unreflectively presupposing that to explain behavioral facts is to give a "deterministic" causal process account of those facts. Thus, they would be inclined to ask "But how is such knowledge possible?"

But we clearly have such knowledge, and, just as clearly, it is not obviously susceptible of a causal process account. If to proceed with concepts which are not demonstrably rendered in causal process terms is open to methodological objection on that score, then so is any such objection and any such question as "But how is such knowledge possible?" for these are not demonstrably capable of being rendered in causal process terms. So, whatever force such questions about our knowledge may have, none needs to be answered prior to conducting an investigation, hence none raises a methodological issue.

Thus, there is a clear line, conceptually, to an adequate conceptual framework for a behavioral science. It would have the general character of a grammar or calculus (without literally being either one) augmented by specific behavioral concepts (the equivalent of a vocabulary relative to a grammar). In this framework, both known and as yet unknown behavioral facts would have a systematic place and relationship to one another. Relative to the conceptual framework which provided formal and systematic access to the subject matter of behavior, the function of a substantive theory would be to specify in an intelligible and general way *which* among the possible behavioral phenomena do in fact occur and which do not. (In general, our present "behavioral" theories do nothing of the sort, but merely give us some language for redescribing some of what we observe.)

B. On Totality and Logical Structure

The difference between the know-nothing intuitionism of a historical, empirical approach and an explicit, calculational approach to the issue of systematizing behavioral possibilities is not the difference between scientific caution and recklessness. Neither is it the difference between grasping some behavioral possibilities and grasping more of them, nor is it some merely quantitative difference between grasping many possibilities and grasping all of them. Rather, what is at issue is the kind of thinking that can be brought to bear on the study of behavior and, correspondingly, the kind of understanding that can be achieved in regard to behavior.

An important example in this regard is a pattern of considerations which I will here designate as a "domain analysis" and a corresponding form of presentation which we may designate as a "domain argument." Although neither is a recent invention, neither the form of analysis nor the form of presentation appears to have been identified and specifically named as a distinctive pattern by the philosophers who might have been expected to do so. By way of clarifying the general character of a domain analysis, I will refer to an example of a domain argument presented by Hans Reichenbach in a lecture some years ago.

Reichenbach begins with the observation that on inspection it seems obvious that the surface of a sphere is a two-dimensional surface. On the other hand, just as obviously, it is not *just* like a flat plane, which is the paradigm of a two-dimensional surface. Thus, we have the normal sort of basis for asking "Well, then, *is* it really a two-dimensional surface?" and "Is there any way of telling?" His answer to the latter is "Yes, there is," and he proceeds as follows:

> Introduce a two-dimensional, orthogonal coordinate system on the flat plane. You will find that every point on that plane has a unique description given by its coordinates within that framework. Now introduce the same coordinate system on the surface of the sphere. (An example of this kind is our system of latitude and longitude on the surface of the earth.) What you will find now is that on this surface there are two "singular" points for which the coordinate system does not provide a unique description. (The two points correspond to "North Pole" and "South Pole" in the case of latitude and longitude.) This shows that

the surface of a sphere is not a two-dimensional surface.

It is important, he cautions, to be clear about what has and what has not been shown here. It is not, for example, that there are two points on the surface of the sphere which are somehow different from all the other points. It is not that there are two points on that surface which, on being identified and closely inspected, can be seen to be singular points. Quite to the contrary, there is no point on the surface of the sphere for which a unique description could not be achieved by means of a two-dimensional rectangular coordinate system. All that would be required to accomplish this result for a particular point would be a suitable choice of a second point to serve as the origin of the coordinate system, and it can be shown that a suitable second point is always available. However, this result can be guaranteed only if the point in question is picked out in advance of the introduction of the coordinate system and if the latter is then introduced ad hoc. Even then, it will be the case that, no matter how we maneuver our introduction of the coordinate system so as to achieve ad hoc applicability, i.e., uniqueness for the pre-selected point, *there will be* two singular points on that surface once we have introduced the coordinate system.

Thus, he concludes, it is not that a two-dimensional rectangular grid is totally inadequate or that it cannot be used for many practical purposes involving the surface of a sphere. But you have to remember that such a practical approach neglects some fundamental aspects of the matter. The surface of a sphere is not really a two-dimensional surface, and a two-dimensional rectangular coordinate system is inadequate in principle, and you may be reminded of that to your sorrow if you proceed in a merely "practical" way. When we consider three-dimensional surfaces, you will see that, although in some ways the description is more complicated, the surface of a sphere can be described as a three-dimensional surface with no "ifs," "ands," or "buts," and because of this, in its own way, that's the *simplest* description.

The point to notice here is that in this example this kind of thinking depends on the intelligibility of talking about the totality of points on the surface of a sphere and in no way depends on any empirical procedure of inspecting or counting any points on a historically observed spherical surface. It is because we have the concept of a sphere and a systematic description available that we are able to talk sensibly about "all the points." The argument could not be carried out if we were restricted to considering "some," "many," or "nearly all" of such points. Further, the argument depends not only on being able to talk about all the points but on considering them all simultaneously. If we violated the simultaneity condition we would be able to "prove" that a two-dimensional coordinate system could provide an adequate representation of the spherical surface, since we could take the points one by one (in principle) and show that each time the ad hoc application of the coordinate system did the job for *that* point. There is no question that each time *a* two-dimensional coordinate system will do the job, but if we proceeded in that way, it would not be the same coordinate system in each case. The argument is not to the effect that the job cannot be done ad hoc for *a* point by *a* two-dimensional orthogonal coordinate system, but rather than no such coordinate system will do the job for the surface of the sphere, i.e., for all of the points simultaneously.

Thus, a domain argument does not deal with particulars (facts, events, objects, etc.) within a domain of facts, but, rather, with what does or does not characterize the domain or what is or is not possible regarding that domain. In Reichenbach's example the conclusion was that the domain in question was characterized by singular elements when it was mapped onto the coordinate system and that since the singularities could not be associated with any particular elements in the domain they implied a lack of fit between the domain and the coordinate system. Psychologists will recognize a family resemblance between the concept of a domain analysis and the statistical concept of "degree of freedom." Philosophers and mathematicians will recognize an even closer resemblance to the established topic of "the difference between 'any' and 'all.' "

The concept of a domain argument has an obvious relevance to the problem of the validity and coherence of references to "all behavior." For example, the following considerations can be regarded as a domain argument.

It is persons of whom it may be said that for every historically actual thought, every piece of theorizing, every observation, every piece of knowledge, and every speculation, hypothesis, investigation, prediction, description, et cetera, there is one such individual for whom it is (has the status of) "*my*" thought, theory, observation, et cetera. (Recall here the discussion of Chronological description in Section III and the relation of that to the pre-empirical basis of empiricism.) Every instance of a behavioral fact is someone's instance, and every view of behavioral facts is someone's view.

Conversely, there is no person for whom *all* thoughts, behaviors, theories, observations, et cetera, are *someone else's* thoughts, etc. Thus, there is no person who *could* make reference to all behaviors, thoughts, etc., by means of a third-person or second-person description because there is no person for whom "all behavior" is identical to "his (her, their, your) behavior." There is no person for whom "all behavior" is not identical with "my behavior *and* your and his and their behavior."

Thus, we have a way of circumscribing the kind of logic and way of talking which could possibly give any of *us* (us persons) access to all behavioral possibilities.

It is not, of course, that it makes no sense to talk about "all" behaviors, thoughts, theories, viewpoints, descriptions, et cetera. Rather, no matter who it is that makes such a reference, it remains the case that "All behavior (thoughts, etc.)" distributes across "my behavior" and "your, his, her, their behavior." Because of this, there are constraints on what any person could say about "all behav-

174

ior" (and anything said about "all behavior" is said *by* some person). Specifically, the constraint on what is said about "all behavior" is that it cannot violate whatever constraints hold for *either* "my behavior" or "his, her, their, your behavior." It follows that a conceptual framework which could possibly give us access to "all behavior" must have a reflexive conceptual structure, since that is the only way that any person can refer to "my behavior."

It might be argued that third-person descriptions include by far the largest proportion of the cases of behavior (thoughts, observations, etc.) since the cases of "my behavior" will be only a small fraction of the total. Thus, third-person descriptions might be claimed to be an adequate approximation to "all behavior" for practical purposes. Such reasoning is, for most practical purposes, illusory. It is comparable to arguing that when it comes to applying orthogonal coordinates to the surface of a sphere, the number of points which can lie off the reference axes is much larger than the number of points which can lie on the axes and that therefore, practically speaking, one can dispense with the reference axes altogether. There is a double absurdity here. First, since the placement of the reference axes is neither fixed nor given, there is *no* point on the surface which could not lie on the reference axes (or the origin, for that matter) and no point which could not lie off the reference axes. Second, the indispensable function of a coordinate system in providing access to the points on the sphere in no way depends on what proportion of the points lie on or off the reference axes. Similarly, *both* "my behavior" and "their (his, her, your) behavior" include all behavior, for there is no behavior which is not, for someone, "my behavior" and, for someone else, "his behavior." Thus, neither is an *approximation* to "all behavior."

Rather, the third-person approach may be regarded as defining an egocentric role. The person who speaks of "all behavior" and means "their behavior" is, in effect, exempting himself implicitly

175

from the regularities and constraints which he attributes to "them." The institutionalization of third-person grammar in traditional behavioral theorizing is, perhaps unwittingly, the institutionalization of such egocentricity. It is often presented as "objectivity."

The notion of approximation can be pursued a little further, given the previous discussion of subject matter. Third-person descriptions can approximate "all behavior" only in the sense that they might "apply to" most behavior. But the subject matter of third-person descriptions is not an approximation to the subject matter of "all behavior" because the range of facts which can be described or asked about in third person is not an approximation to the range of behavioral facts which can be formulated or asked about. There are a variety of well-known asymmetries between first-person and third-person descriptions which preclude the possibility of ignoring either kind.

The requirement of reflexivity has not been totally ignored in the recent history of psychology, but it has been frequently misunderstood and frequently mispresented. Likewise, efforts to meet the requirement have most commonly been futile or disingenuous.

The requirement has sometimes been presented as the requirement for a theory to account for the theorist's own theoretical behavior. And the response of some theorists (e.g., Skinner, 1957) has been to try to show that their theories do that. One has to wonder why it has seemed to be any sort of challenge to a theorist to be asked to talk specifically about himself in the technical language with which he talks about everyone (or all organisms). Of course, it can be done, particularly in technical and theoretical language. But for a deterministic theory doing this is a violation of the simultaneity condition mentioned above, and it is the equivalent of taking the points on the sphere one by one and showing that in each case the ad hoc introduction of a two-dimensional rectangular coordinate system will do the job. If a theory states or implies that the occurrence of a behavior is simply the deterministic consequence of antecedent conditions, there is no question that the theorist may "say" that this is so about his own theorizing and he may even mention some number of specific antecedents. However, the question at issue is not whether he can later say this about his theorizing but whether his theorizing *could be* what the theory implies all behavior is, i.e., the deterministic consequence of antecedent conditions. The answer to that was given in the examination of "determinism" per se and will hold for any theory incorporating a deterministic ideology. The conclusion there that "None of us is really one of us" is the discursive equivalent of saying (with numbers) that the North Pole is at a given longitude, but it is also somewhere else (at another longitude). We are us, but also we are really someone else. Thus, such a "demonstration" of "the application of the theory to the theorist" may be an occasion for amusement, irritation, sadness, contempt, or other condign response, but hardly for any serious discussion. After all, the requirement was that the theory *account for* the theorist's behavior, not that it merely be used in talking about that behavior. For that, the behavior would have to be subject matter and not merely the locus of application.

The situation is just as clear-cut, though perhaps not as obvious, when, instead of a scientific theorist talking about his own scientific theorizing, we have a philosophical theorist talking about someone's scientific theorizing. This case is historically important because it is standard practice for behavioral scientists to appeal to "the scientific method" and ultimately to "the philosophy of science" when the legitimacy of their procedures is questioned. What should be clear, however, is that, when it comes to a theory which purports to hold for all behavior, it does not make any difference who it is that talks about the theorist's theorizing. There is no question that a philosopher can say what philosophers say about scientific theorizing and that the scientific theorist can say of his and the philosopher's theorizing what he says of all behavior. The question at issue is not whether each can say what he says, but whether the theorizing of either *could be* what the scientist's theory says or implies that all behavior is. For our traditional "naturalistic" behavior theories, the answer is "No."

If we pursue the matter a little further, in a diagnostic vein, we may detect a reason, albeit a mistaken one, for the popularity of the third-person approach in our recent history. The background facts are (1) that our most dogmatic proponents of "objectivity" have almost invariably been also proponents of "determinism" and (2) that a dogmatic and doctrinal theology predisposes one to the active detection and correction of sin. It has apparently seemed to these practitioners that to give any explicit recognition to "my behavior" when talking about "all behavior" is to claim that "my behavior" is in principle different from everybody else's and, more specifically, that it is somehow exempt from the divine necessity which grips us all with an iron hand. We hear the undertone of this belief in the query, mentioned earlier, of "Where, in the chain of physiological events, is there a place for volition to enter in and affect the causal sequence?" And we hear the clang and echo of the Inquisitor's tools in the passage by Minsky.

There is indeed a singularity of some sort in talking about "my behavior," and our Inquisitor is sensitive to it. The mistake that he makes here is to suppose that an *irregularity* of some kind is at issue. That is comparable to supposing that when we comment on the singular points created by the *match* between the rectangular coordinate system and the surface of the sphere we are claiming that there are two points on the sphere which are intrinsically and already different from the others. That would be an irregularity indeed. But also, in that case, the sphere would not be a sphere, and so we reject the notion of an irregularity. Since we reject the irregularities, we are able to use the corresponding singularities as a basis for rejecting the framework and procedure which produced them. Thus, we see this use of rectangular coordinates here as being in principle a distortion of reality, and the reality in question is the sphere and its structure. The rectangular coordinate system is not *false*; it is merely a failure.

The determinist does it otherwise. He, too, rejects the notion of irregularity, but he does it, as we have seen, by shifting his ground ad hoc. Because of this, he interprets any refusal to shift one's ground as an assertion of irregularities, and he correctly perceives the refusal to talk about oneself in the third person as just such a refusal to shift one's ground.

> Gil: "I don't talk about other people as though *I* were someone else. Why, then, should I have to talk about myself as though I were someone else? How could I claim to be special in this most extraordinary way? Impossible! Ridiculous! Bah! Humbug! . . . "

Thus, proponents of causal determinism have taken all objections as being claims, in one form or another, that there is somewhere an indeterminancy in the machinery. What they face, however, is not sin, but heresy. The objection is not that there is somewhere a non-deterministic flaw in the machinery, but rather that the whole machinery approach to dealing with *all* behavior in principle is intellectually naive and laughable and might well be judged to be utterly without any redeeming social, artistic, or scientific value.

Although it is not as prominent currently as it has been in recent decades, there is another well-known methodological position for which the concepts presented above are also relevant and which, therefore, bears some mention. That is the position that, although you have to make some assumptions in order to proceed with scientific theorizing or experimentation, there is nothing necessarily arbitrary or merely dogmatic about the procedure because each such

179

assumption can itself be tested on a different occasion by not assuming it there but making other assumptions instead. I have argued elsewhere that in such a case there can be no presumption that what is assumed in the one case is the same thing as what is tested in the other case, since there is no way to know what the relation between the two sets of assumptions is. If both sets of assumptions can be fitted into a more inclusive framework then the problem is resolved for the first two but arises anew with respect to the third. The limit of such a progression is an all-inclusive metaphysical position which is not any less arbitrary or dogmatic than less-inclusive positions. Given the concept of a domain analysis and the Reichenbach example, it should be clear that the position that "You can test an assumption by making other assumptions on other occasions" is just another version of shifting one's ground ad hoc. From such an approach, therefore, no grasp of the fundamentals of *all* behavior could be expected.

Let us return to the notion of constraints on first-person and third-person descriptions and the asymmetries between them. Consider that although it is quite possible to say of him that "He is now mistaken in what he takes to be the case" it becomes nonsensical if it is transposed into "I am now mistaken in what I take to be the case." Because of this, it will be equally nonsensical to say of all behavior that it involves the individual being mistaken in what he takes to be the case. The same will hold for weaker forms such as "never really knows what's the case" or "is in principle biased in his judgment," both of which are almost invariably implied by our familiar theories. Similarly, "He is not saying anything now" becomes nonsensical if it is changed to "I am not saying anything now" and therefore is also nonsensical in the form "Nobody is saying anything now" (or, "ever"). In both of these first-person cases and universal cases uttering those words will not succeed in saying anything. This feature was exemplified in the degradation ceremony analysis of "determinism." The third-person description "None of them is one of us" can succeed; the first-person form "None of us is one of us" must fail. The analysis of determinism can now be seen as a special case or a particular version of the domain argument concerning "all behavior."

C. ON NATURALISM AND REFLEXIVITY

Issues concerning first-person and third-person description have played an important part in the history of science, though this fact has been relatively unpublicized. Traditionally, the practices of "behavioral science" have been carried on by practitioners who have accepted the principle (urged on them by all and sundry, but especially by philosophers of science and "natural science" practitioners) that behavioral science must consist of the "application" of a transcendent "method" to a merely nominally specified subject matter, something *called* "behavior," *whatever that might turn out to be* (upon the application of the method). These practitioners have been neither neutral nor impartial in their choice of idiom and implicit logic. They have taken great care to avoid being in the position of having to refer "subjectively" to any such phenomenon as "my" behavior, beliefs, et cetera. Instead, they have (apparently confusing an impersonal idiom with an objective methodology) adopted an impersonal, third-person idiom (even to the point of using the passive voice in reporting experimental procedures). This choice has taken the form, among others, of talking about ("all") behavior from the implied vantage point of the hypothetical, disembodied, "objective" observer whose own behavioral character never enters the picture as such and for whom, therefore, all behavior is "their" behavior. Since there is no such vantage point, no such observer, and no such status, there can be no such view of "all behavior," but only the pretence of it, and so there are difficulties. ("Of course, no description or theory could be *really* objective, but. . . . " This line of thought ends with "and so I have to suppose myself to be mistaken in what I think now.")

The difficulties can be characterized succinctly by reference to the concepts presented in Section II. Specifically, we shall need the concept of the "world" of possible facts generated by the "ultimate objects" of a theory or conceptual system. Each such "world" is limited absolutely by the concepts and logical structure of the corresponding theory or conceptual system. In "the world of biology," for example, there is no possible fact concerning the esthetic, economic, or ethical characteristics of an object. In that "world," no such object as an esthetic object or an economic object could be a real object. Rather, such objects as these could at best have a ghostly sort of existence there, and facts about those objects would have an equally wraithlike character. A similar result would hold for "Person." Clearly there is no possible place for a human object in the world of biology, chemistry, physics, or any of the traditional "natural" sciences. Just as clearly, though this fact has seldom received any commentary, there is no place for a Person in the world of psychoanalysis, the world of operant conditioning, the world of systems theory, the world of rote-memory learning, or any of the traditional "naturalistic" theories within the behavioral sciences.

This conclusion can be drawn directly by inspection of each such theory, but there is also a general explanation for the incompatibility. What is constitutive of such theorizing is that it is some variation on the clockwork model of the universe. That is, such theorizing is based on the presupposition that the fundamental facts of the domain in question consist of "deterministic" causal processes which operate in a medium consisting of structures of some sort (physiological, cognitive, social, etc.). Any such theorizing, no matter whether its idiom be physiological, cognitive, social, biological, physical, theological, or whatever, will, when taken literally and seriously as a theory of human behavior, involve the same nonsensical postures as "determinism" itself. Since "None of us is really one of us" no deterministic "world" will have a place for any of *us*.

As it happens, although persons cannot have a place within "naturalistic" theories or models, they are an essential requirement of such theories or models. If they cannot have a place within those theories and their corresponding worlds, then they must have an external relation to such theories and such worlds. For theories are bodies of statements, and no such set of statements is per se guaranteed to have any greater or closer connection to the real world than does the most bizarre of fantasies. And, as I commented initially, no body of statements can confer a methodological status on itself. No less than "Person," all methodological facts about a theory lie outside the scope of the theory. The worlds of biology, psychoanalysis, stimulus-response, chemistry, et cetera, have no possible place for "theory," "description," "explanation," "confirmation," and so forth. They have no possible place for theories, either, not even biological, psychoanalytic, stimulus-response, or chemical theories.

It is only in the real world, the behavioral world (LC-I) that theories have a methodological value and a place of any kind. It is by persons that they are constructed, and it is for persons alone that they may have some value, and it is in the world of persons alone that they can have a place. In this way, persons are the *sine qua non* of our "naturalistic" theories and the corresponding "worlds." Persons have no place within the worlds of physics, biology, stimulus-response, psychoanalysis, et al., because it is the latter worlds which must presuppose the world of persons and their behavior in order to have a place and hence a degree of reality.

These conclusions are not controversial, I take it, but the re-

183

minder may be to the point here. The facts in question have been codified in the "humanistic" discipline of philosophy of science. The world of philosophy of science is another one which lies outside the worlds of physics, biology, stimulus-response, psychoanalysis, et al. It also lies outside the world of philosophy of science. (Philosophy of science provides nonscientific theories of the behavior of scientists; it provides no corresponding account of the behavior of philosophers of science.)

I mention this because one of the most predictable sorts of reaction to the preceding formulation would be an indignant recital of the values of scientific theories, their empirical justification, et cetera, in short, some repetition of a few lines from some philosophical theory of science. I have no doubt that some sort of apology could be given for traditional scientific theorizing. The only point here, however, is just that any such apology, together with the necessity for such an apology and the criteria of its success or failure in various respects, will lie outside the conceptual scope of these scientific theories. Hence such theories and their corresponding "worlds" have no intrinsic value, are essentially incomplete, and cannot stand on their own in any respect whatever. Persons are essential.

In short, what lies outside the scope of traditional "naturalistic" third-person psychological theorizing is the essential and distinctive subject matter of behavioral science. These theories are essentially formulations of some type of deterministic machinery, and in order for that machinery to be operative there is required an individual (the person, scientist, observer, thinker, experimenter, listener, explainer, etc.) external to the conceptual and factual scope of the theory. In the world created by the use of the theory by persons, such an individual could have no real existence, but only a paradoxical and insubstantial sort of existence. Given these features, it seems historically apt to characterize the difficulty with such theories as "the problem of the ghost outside the machine."

An explanation which requires such a ghost will be a supernatural explanation, not a naturalistic one. The "unbiased, objective observer" is one version of the ghost outside the machine, and the requirement of such a ghost is the behavioral equivalent of the singularities produced by the inadequate coordinate system on the surface of the sphere. Behavioral accounts of this sort are inadequate in principle because they fail to do even elementary justice to the facts of behavior.

Since it is the historical tradition of "naturalism" which has led to such results, we must either reconsider what it is that would constitute a naturalistic approach to behavior or else relegate naturalism to the heap of superstitions and outmoded folklore in the history of science, along with reductionism, operationalism, determinism, skepticism, and others.

If, instead of merely following historical custom, we take a methodological view of the matter, it seems obvious that we take "naturalism" not as the name for a historically familiar style of theorizing, but as the polar contrast to "supernaturalism." (Similarly, we take "up" as the contrast to "down" rather than as the name of a particular direction.) And from that vantage point it seems equally clear that naturalism is in no sense equivalent to determinism, technology, reductionism, clockwork models of the universe, or anything of the sort.

Rather, to adopt a "naturalistic" position is to reject certain kinds of mystery (e.g., "God's will," "mere coincidence," "a miracle," "brute fact") as being finally explanatory, and perhaps to reject them as being explanatory principles at all (see below). It is, therefore, to endorse, and sometimes to seek for, an adequate logical connection (not to be confused with a deductive relation) between what is to be explained and what qualifies as an explanation of *it*. The judgment that supernatural accounts exhibit a deficit of this sort is what is historically reflected in "naturalism" as a methodological stance.

Of course, history has its own ironies and accidents. For example, Hempel, who might be characterized as an apostle of "naturalism" in behavioral science, urges "covering laws" upon us as the epitome of successful empirical behavioral science. Under this view we would typically employ the following verbal formula: "This A caused this B because this A is an X and this B is a Y, so it's a case of an X causing a Y, *and they all do that.*" The final clause in the formula is what purportedly carries the explanatory force. But this clause is classifiable as one of our mysteries. For example, it could be regarded as one version of "brute fact" or "mere coincidence (that they all do that)." And mysteries are like contradictions or null classes in logic, essentially interchangeable, since they differ only in the form of representation. Thus, we should have to ask whether adding *"and they all do that"* is an improvement over *"and that is the will of God"* or even different from it. The latter has at least the practical virtue of reminding us that the ritual intonation of such formulas will not preclude our being surprised some day by our observations of A's and B's or X's and Y's. The two formulations have a closer connection than just both being mysteries, however. "And they all do that" is a thematic variant of "and it just happens to be necessary," which, as we saw earlier, can be understood as the truncated and secularized version of "and that is the will of God." In this way, the Hempelian phrasing can be seen as a local version of an outmoded theological paradox.

Just as replacing a ghost inside the machine with a ghost outside the machine will not convert a supernatural explanation into a naturalistic one, neither will a change from an overtly theological language to a secular idiom accomplish this result. Thus, ironically, that style of theorizing which has been most aggressively advertised as "naturalistic" and "scientific" can be seen to be supernaturalistic in the sense developed above. I do not believe there is another current sense of "naturalism" which would be relevant as a criterion for scientific practice.

Of course, I do not mean to suggest that there is no value in being told that the copper pipe expanded when the blowtorch was applied because this was a case of a metal being heated. Rather, whatever explanatory value such a statement may have must be contained in the statement itself, for it will not be generated by such additions as "and they all do that," "and that is the will of God," "and that is the nature of such things," et cetera.

In actual practice, one would have to suppose, these latter expressions have pretty much the same force as "That is what is to be expected; it would require an explanation if the piece of metal (the pipe) did *not* expand." Note, however, that this latter is not part of any explanation at all; still less is it one. Rather, it is a conventional way of assigning the methodological status of "explanation" to the statement that this A caused this B because it's a case of an X causing a Y.

It might be argued that, then, this is a way of bringing methodological and substantive facts together and should therefore be considered desirable in light of my introductory comments. However, the appearance here is misleading, just as the apparently substantive clause ("and they all do that," "and that is its nature," etc.) is misleading. What is being accomplished here in this misleading way is that both a substantive move (the description) and a methodological move (the status assignment) are accomplished in the same sentence. That is hardly a case of bringing the two kinds of facts within a single logical domain. If that can be done at all, it can be done openly and systematically, not merely verbally and implicitly.

D. On Being Informative about Something

From a historical viewpoint it may well seem perplexing that despite the fixed intention on the part of an army of interested persons to study behavior scientifically, our "behavioral" theories have no place for persons, behavior, or the rest of the distinctive subject matter of behavioral science. Failures of this magnitude call for some explanation, else the perplexity might well become incredulity, and with some reason. Of course, no single or simple explanation will be historically adequate in regard to such an extensive and complex set of events. It will be of interest, however, to delineate some paradigmatic forms of explanation in this connection. The further value of such a presentation is that it may help to identify further issues to be resolved or difficulties to be avoided by a behavioral science.

Let us consider in crude outline the task of formulating and communicating some new information about something. (This, after all, will be one of the central tasks of any science.) For this purpose, we may begin with the subject-predicate sentence, which historically far antedates science, just as the task of formulating and communicating information about something far antedates science.

If we are to communicate something about something, we clearly have two tasks, i.e., to identify what we are talking about and to say something about it (or characterize or describe it.) These are the basic and familiar functions of subject and predicate constructions in a sentence. Let us survey some of the possibilities of success and failure, and of confusion, disagreement, and nonsense which follow from the fact that there are two tasks rather than one and that they are these two particular tasks.

1. It is clearly desirable not to confuse a case of identifying a subject matter with a case of saying something about it. In natural

188

language, accordingly, we have fairly distinctive forms of expression and structural constraints so that subjects are seldom confused with predicates in the same sentence. In general, either distinctive terminology or distinctive grammatical forms could accomplish the task of preventing confusion between identifying and characterizing subject matter. The use of technical (e.g., theoretical) terminology for the characterization of a subject matter is a conventional device for reducing ambiguity between identification and characterization of a subject matter.

2. If no special conventions are adopted there will be possibilities for terms to be interchangeable, as between identification and characterization. For example:

(a) The filing cabinet   is black.
(b) The black filing cabinet   has four drawers.
(c) The black, four-drawer filing cabinet
                                  is made of metal.
(d) The black, metal, four-drawer filing cabinet etc.

3. The identification of subject matter may be given by a "purely referring" utterance. For example:

(a) This   is a filing cabinet.
(b) Number 36A   has four drawers.
(c) Paul   has a brother, Peter.

I speak of "utterance" here rather than "term" or "expression" because utterances are historical particulars whereas the others, being forms of utterance, are not. The same expression may on one occasion be used in a purely referring way and on another occasion not. A purely referring utterance is one which identifies without any characterization.

4. In normal communication it is not always clear whether the subject matter identification is being accomplished by a purely

referring utterance or not. It is not always clear whether a given utterance is intended to be purely referential or not. For example:

(a) *Gil:* Let's buy that filing cabinet to put our papers in.
    Wil: But we need something with drawers.
    Gil: I said "filing cabinet," didn't I?

(b) *Gil:* Lend me that filing cabinet you bought yesterday.
    Wil: I didn't buy anything yesterday. I bought a filing cabinet last week.
    Gil: Come on, now. You know which one I mean.

(c) *Gils* Let's use No. 36A to put our papers in.
    Wil: We can't. You know it belongs to Paul.

5. In characterizing a subject matter, the subject matter is presupposed, or taken as "given" (in the geometric sense, not, e.g., as a "perceptual given"), for the sake of the characterization. Because of this, a description which is otherwise questionable may be acceptable for the purpose of identification (see example (b) above).

6. The use of a purely referential identification of subject matter will formally reduce to zero the scope of what must be presupposed or taken as "given." It will therefore maximize the range of possible characterizations. For example, "This black filing cabinet is black" is a tautology, whereas "This filing cabinet is black" is informative and is a possible empirical finding. So also is "This is a black filing cabinet."

7. Utterances which, by either convention or intention, are purely referring utterances will not succeed in identifying a subject matter except within a body of social practices and a known historical context. Thus:

(a) *Gil:* I'm thinking of something.
    Wil: Thinking of what?
    Gil: What I'm thinking of (or "just something").
    Wil: Stop wasting my time.

(b) *Gil:* This one looks like a good filing cabinet. I'll buy it.
    Wil: Which one?
    Gil: This one.
    Wil: Oh, you mean the black, four-drawer one?
    Gil: No, this one.
    Wil: Oh, you mean the one nearest to you?
    Gil: Of course.

8. Therefore the making of a purely referential utterance for identifying subject matter is an empty formality, methodologically speaking, since it will be replaceable by a descriptive sort of identification (see 7 (b)). The primacy of the descriptive identification is shown by the fact that some characterizations will result in a rejection of either the characterization or the identification. For example:

(a) *Gil (pointing to a blotter on a desk):* This is over five feet tall.
    Wil: Anyone can see it isn't.

(b) *Gil (pointing):* This is later than 5:00 o'clock.
    Jil(to Wil): What's he talking about?
    Wil: I thought at first he was talking about the blotter, but obviously he isn't.
    Jil: Then what is he talking about?
    Wil: God only knows. Whatever it may be that can be later than 5:00 o'clock, I suppose. Maybe he's talking about a train or a radio program.

Jil: Then what does he mean "this"?

Wil: Would it be any better if he said "that"? You'd better be careful with him.

9. If there were utterances which really were purely referential there would be no way of knowing or deciding what the subject matter was. (In part, this is the issue, discussed in Section IV, of "What action is it that these two descriptions are supposed to be descriptions *of?*" It is also the problem of "bare particulars" in the history of Western thought. And it is the issue of subject matter versus locus of study or application.) In this case, at best, the characterization would have to do double duty as identification. ("Then what's he talking about?" "God only knows. Whatever it may be that can be later than 5:00 o'clock, I suppose.")

10. The identification of subject matter may be accomplished by a locution which is irrelevant to the characterization (is of a different logical category, lies within a different conceptual system). In this case, most of the advantages of a purely referential utterance will be preserved. For example:

(a) *Gil:*   What's the price of this near cabinet as compared with the far one?

    Wil: Two dollars less. It's 28 dollars and the other is 30.

(b) *Gil:*   What's the price of the 28 dollar cabinet as compared with the 30 dollar one?

    Wil: If you know that, what are you asking?

Note that the identification in (a) serves its purpose admirably precisely because the position of the cabinets is irrelevant to their price, hence nothing about the price has to be presupposed in framing the question, thus providing an alternative to the absurdity of (b).

192

11. Identification via an irrelevant (in the sense of number 10, above) locution is the identification of a locus rather than a logical subject matter. In a general or systematic formulation it will drop out completely, since it is not what the characterization is *about*. Thus, "Are near filing cabinets generally more expensive than far ones?" is a nonsensical "question."

12. Identification of subject matter may be accomplished by reference to something which, though distinct from the characterization, is not irrelevant to it. For example:

Gil: What's the price of the black filing cabinet as compared to the orange one?

Wil: The orange one is 30 dollars; the black one is 2 dollars less.

In a general or systematic formulation this kind of identifying reference need not drop out. When it does not, some opportunity for explanation is usually present. For example:

Gil: Why does the orange one cost more?

Wil: Colored enamel is more expensive and harder to get on properly.

Gil: *That* much more expensive? *That* much harder?

Wil: Yes.

Gil: Are colored filing cabinets generally more expensive?

Wil: Yes, and that's why.

Gil: So they all do that.

Wil: Huh?

Gil: Never mind.

13. Identification of subject matter may be made by a reference which is neither irrelevant in the sense of number 10 nor distinct

in the sense of number 12, but is simply more general or more extensive or both. (This was the nature of the "informative" solution to "What action is it that these two descriptions are descriptions of?") In this case the opportunity is present for question and answer, but in this case the answer will be only that and not an explanation. Thus:

> *Gil:* What's the price of this cabinet?
> *Wil:* Twenty-eight dollars.
> *Gil:* I'll take it.

Here, "price" implies a monetary unit and a number, hence "28 dollars" merely specifies *which* already known to be possible price is the price of this cabinet. In contrast, the "why" in "Why does the orange one cost more?" does not imply anything about labor or paint costs. Thus, the answer which mentions these two things goes beyond the content of the question in a way which at face value qualifies it as an explanation.

14. "Explanation" is not a characteristic of locutions but of utterances within the context of certain personal interactions. For example:

> (a) *Gil:* What reason did John have to say that?
>   *Wil:* He was angry at you.

> (b) *Gil:* Why did John say that?
>   *Wil:* He was angry at you.

> (a) *Gil:* How many pairs of shoes does he have in his closet?
>   *Wil:* He has 22 pairs of shoes in his closet.

> (b) *Gil:* Why did she berate him so?
>   *Wil:* He has 22 pairs of shoes in his closet.

194

In the examples (a) Wil's reply is merely an answer. In (b) the "same" answer is an explanation. Compare:

> (c) *Gil:* Why did this pipe expand when I put the blow-torch to it?
>
> *Wil:* Well, there's no reason why a pipe would have to expand under these circumstances, and lots of them won't. Forget about this whole pipe business. *That's irrelevant.* What you're calling a case of a pipe expanding when you put a blowtorch to it is in fact a case of a metal expanding when heated. And, of course, that's what you would expect. So if you look at it that way, no question arises and nothing needs explaining.

Here we notice that, although (c) fits the same discursive form as (b), Wil's reply in (c) is not straightforwardly an explanation in the way that his reply in (b) is an explanation. Indeed, Wil's reply in (c) is not even an answer to Gil's question. Instead, his reply is a rejection of Gil's question and a plea-bargaining move in regard to the subject matter. Wil proposes that they talk about *this* rather than *that*. Note that in neither case of (b) does Wil's reply amount to this. Saying "He was angry at you" would be unintelligible if it was preceded by "Forget about John's saying that. That's irrelevant." And it would be incoherent to add in this case "If you look at it this way, no question arises and nothing needs explaining." John's saying that is intelligible because there are intelligible patterns (of behavior and relationships) in which it could have a place. "He was angry at you" is explanatory because it identifies such a pattern. In contrast, in (c) no such relationship holds. If "metals expand when heated" is taken as an observational generalization, then that fact is in the same logical domain as "the pipe expanded" but the connection is not sufficiently close to generate an explanation (its being a pipe is *irrelevant*). If "metals expand when heated" is taken as a derivation within thermodynamics, then it is not in the same logical domain as "the pipe expanded." The world of thermodynamics not only has no place for persons, it also has no place for material objects such as plumbers' pipe.

In short, just as only physical facts can simply and directly explain or be explained by physical facts, behavioral facts can be explained only by behavioral facts. To "explain" a behavioral fact by reference to a physical fact is to change the subject (an event within the behavioral domain), and it will remain a change of subject even when the change carries with it some practical advantage (within the behavioral domain).

The foregoing considerations may be regarded as an elaboration of the reminder that a naturalistic explanation requires an appropriate logical connection between what is explained and what could explain it. We might, at this point, hear some historical echoes: "Forget about Johnny sassing the teacher. What we have here is a conditioned response which . . . "; "Forget about his washing his hands all the time. What we have here is a case of instinctual energies barely held in check by a fragile ego which. . . . "

A survey of the foregoing considerations which are involved in the general task of identifying a subject matter and saying something about it makes it relatively easy to see the traditional forms of scientific theorizing in certain ways:

(a) The attempt has been to be as noncommittal as possible in identifying subject matter in order (in accordance with number 6, above) to maximize the possibilities of empirical findings. The attempt has been implemented by using ordinary language ("observation language") either in a purportedly purely referring way (see numbers 3 and 6, above) or as an irrelevant locution (see number 10, above). (This is why it has been possible to say with a straight face and clear conscience, "I'm studying something called 'behavior', whatever that may turn out to be.")

(b) The attempt has been to minimize ambiguity (see number 2, above) between identification and characterization of subject matter. The attempt has been implemented by the adoption of special, technical (e.g., theoretical) terminology for the purpose of characterization (see number 1, above). This convention has seemed essential because the problem of ambiguity is magnified tremendously when we put the problem in the context of a historical discipline rather than a single sentence. A historical discipline requires considerable communication among persons and involves cumulative efforts at achieving a systematic, general account of the subject matter.

(c) A further basis for the concern with keeping identification and characterization unambiguously separate lies in the working principle that the characterization should be provisional and changeable (on the basis of empirical evidence) whereas the subject matter identification should be constant. Were the subject matter not constant, there would be nothing for us to change our minds *about*. (Note here the same sort of issue as "What action is it that these two descriptions are descriptions *of*?")

(d) The attempt to ensure unequivocal separation of identification and characterization of subject matter has resulted in a different sort of equivocation and a corresponding dilemma. The equivocation concerns whether in the identification of subject matter the ordinary language expression (e.g., "behavior") which accomplishes this is used in a purely referring way.

(*i*) The classic know-nothing approach corresponds to the use of "behavior" in a purely referring way. Since "behavior" is used in this way, no set of empirical findings about "behavior" is ruled out in advance, and no facts about behavior are known in advance (hence the designation "know-nothing"). So far, so good. The consequences, however, may be less welcome. Since no set of findings (or resultant conclusions) are ruled out no subject matter has been identified, and "behavior" drops out as irrelevant (per number 1 or number 11, above) in our (theoretical) systematizations based on data. What has happened, then, is the creation of a new subject matter, i.e., the "world" defined by the concepts of the technical theory or model. Then such a theory has nothing to say about behavior. ("Then what's he talking about?" "God only knows. Whatever it is that can be 'conditioned' to 'stimuli', I suppose. You'd better be careful with him.")

(*ii*) The "explanatory" value of the theory or model depends on the identification of subject matter *not* being made in a purely referential way. The theory "explains" the subject matter by reformulating the facts of that logical domain, or "world," in a general and systematic way. If there were no prior formulation, there would be nothing to be explained, and our theories would be merely descriptions of their own distinctive subject matter in the same way that references to "foul ball," "home run," "strikeout," et cetera, are merely descriptive of the subject matter of which those same concepts are constitutive. (In saying that such concepts are constitutive of baseball, I mean that the applicability of these concepts to a phenomenon is a logical prerequisite for that phenomenon to be a case of baseball. Were these concepts not applicable we might still have some phenomenon, but it *couldn't* be baseball.) The explanatory value of a theory depends on such conditions as these and not on the form of expression in which its "explanations" are couched (see number 14, above).

(*iii*) It is part of the folklore of the practitioners of "behavioral science" that there is a prior formulation of the subject matter and that this formulation not only antedates, but also competes with scientific accounts and is ultimately to be replaced by the latter. ("Forget about this business of Johnny deciding not to sass the teacher. What we have here is . . . ") Very often this prior formulation is considered to be self-contradictory. ("Absence makes the heart grow fonder"; "Out of sight, out of mind." See Ossorio (1966a) for another view of the matter.) In any case, this prior formulation is universally derogated among scientists with such designations as "folk psychology," "naive psychological theorizing," "prescientific thinking," "implicit personality theory," and others. If we ask *What* is it that these prior formulations are formulations *of?"* we are left with seemingly no alternative but to say "behavior" (whatever that might turn out to be) in a purely referring way, since (a) any existing content of the term will be part of "folk psychology," hence it will be not identification, but characterization, and (b) our own "scientific" formulations are characterizations rather than identifications, and provisional ones at that. But that leads us back to the other horn of the dilemma, namely, that then our "scientific" formulations of "behavior" have nothing to say about behavior.

From a historical perspective such collective misfortune is understandable. Practitioners must always work within the limits of their intellectual traditions and the social structure of their professional activities. What at one time is an intelligent choice among alternatives later becomes a faux pas when one of the relevant methodological issues has been more completely worked through. And wrong choices may result in insoluble dilemmas.

But merely to repeat within our current practices those ways of thinking and acting which are part of our historical tradition would be to present our future historians with a picture of extraordinary naivete: naivete, for example, concerning empiricism. Naivete in supposing that empiricism could possibly be a sovereign principle instead of being always and everywhere limited by and founded upon pre-empirical conceptual principles. Naivete, fostered by philosophers of science, in supposing that all of what is more or less common knowledge about behavior is either empirical or theoretical (or that it is either inductive or deductive). Naivete in supposing that the replacement of one way of talking by another makes the latter an explanation of whatever we talk about in the former. And naivete in supposing or, more likely, presupposing, that the logic of scientific "explanation" as we have known it is an adequate model of either the real world or the real life of actual persons.

Possibly the crucial point, without which the others might have remained harmless, is the second, which is part of the basis for the equivocation noted above. Had there been a clear understanding that most of what we commonly say about behavior and persons generally is definitional, calculational, and performative rather than inductive, theoretical, and descriptive, there would have been little opportunity for supporting the illusion that a completely noncommittal identification of the subject matter of behavior could be given. As it is, our traditional "behavioral science" is founded on errors as fundamental as supposing that it is merely an inductive generalization that "outs" and "at-bats" occur in baseball, that it is explanatory folk theorizing to say that three strikes constitutes an "out," and that what we have hitherto called "baseball" may someday be empirically shown to be something else instead, e.g., a court-martial, a spelling bee, a set of conditioned responses, or a discharge of instinctual energy.

Can we, then, achieve a science of behavior rather than settling cynically, innocently, or dispiritedly for a science of conditioned responses, or of organismic processes, phenomenological machinery, information processing, or other such subject matter? To accomplish a science of behavior we would have to take behavior as a subject matter, not as a dispensable mere way of talking. We would have to recognize that there really is such a thing as the behavior of persons and study that rather than something else. This would also involve recognizing that the conduct of behavioral science is part of the subject matter, not merely a locus of application, and that "my behavior" is no less behavior than "their behavior." It would involve recognizing that some phenomena are cases of behavior and others are not, that in order for a phenomenon to be a case of behavior it must satisfy certain pre-empirical constraints, and that any empirical findings and conclusions concerning behavior are founded on those conceptual requirements, hence not every finding or conclusion is a possible finding or conclusion about the behavior of persons.

Of course it is possible to do all this. We may elaborate this possibility by reexamining the issue of identification and characterization of subject matter in light of some of the conceptual and methodological resources presented earlier.

First, we may note that the technical requirement for distinctive identification and characterization has already been dealt with in a formal, or notational, way. The descriptive formats presented in Section III are specifically designed for the identification and characterization of subject matter. The notational differentiation of "Name" and "Description" correspond directly to the functions of identifying and characterizing.

Second, it should be noted that in the descriptive formats, "Name" implies neither a purely referential identification nor any particular form of locution. All that is required is that the locution used be adequate to the task of achieving the identification. Since, as we have seen, characterization is indispensable for the task of identification, we may as well say that "Name" consists of an identifying characterization.

201

Third, we should note that the standard use of the descriptive formats in identification and characterization is in crucial respects the exact opposite of what I have presented as the traditional approach to these two tasks. In the traditional approach, the identification carries as little content as possible and the characterization *adds* to it substantively. In the (impossible) limiting case, the identification carries no content and the characterization carries all of the information in the combination. In contrast, the standard use of the descriptive formats involves an identification which implies *all* of the relevant possibilities, leaving it to the characterization to *subtract* some of those possibilities, thereby leaving the remaining possibilities to encompass "what is the case." In the (not impossible) limiting case, the identification implies all the logical possibilities, thus providing the maximum possible scope for (empirical) characterization.

The contrast between the two approaches corresponds to the contrast between reductive and holistic approaches discussed in Section V. "To say that a degradation took place here this morning is to say that, of all the courses the history of the world might have taken here then, it took this one." In this formulation, "the course taken by the history of the world here then" provides an identification which offers no empirical constraints on what we might say. The reference to "degradation ceremony" provides such constraints Thus, the standard use of the descriptive formats corresponds to the formulation in number 13, above, i.e., identification is accomplished by a reference which is more general or more extensive (or both) than the characterization. We may designate this procedure as "holistic description."

The two cases of holistic description (more general, more extensive) were discussed above in connection with "Brutus killed Caesar." "What Brutus did was to kill Caesar with a knife" exemplifies the former. "Brutus' killing Caesar with a knife in the

Forum on the Ides of March is the action which both 'Brutus killed Caesar' and 'Brutus killed Caesar with a knife' are descriptions *of*" exemplifies the latter. We saw there that the former is informative whereas the latter is not. It is therefore the former which would be paradigmatic for scientific description. Ironically, the "topic neutral" notion developed by the Identity theorists (and exemplified by "What's going on in the next room is . . . " or "What's happening in his brain is . . . ") is an example of holistic descriptions.

To anticipate a future discussion, we may say here that a holistic description or discourse introduces its subject matter not by being noncommittal, but by placing it somewhere in the empirical scheme of things ("The history of the world was . . . "; "What happened in the experiment was . . . "). Thus, identification is accomplished by a status assignment, albeit not usually a methodological one. Holistic description therefore provides an automatic corrective (though not one that is guaranteed to be effective) to our historical tendency to proliferate subject matters in an intellectual and pragmatic vacuum by reifying our topics of conversation into recondite object or process entities (thoughts, systems, thinking, learning, information processing, metabolizing, experiencing, etc.) which we then study instead of persons and their behavior and which then raise problems for us of "synthesis" or, failing that, reduction to some least common denominator.

Here a reminder is perhaps in order, based on earlier discussion, that reductive systematization offers no resources for explanation, measurement, experimentation, prediction, application, et cetera, that are not available in a holistic systematization. To this we may now add that a holistic approach does open up a possibility which has not been available via the traditional reductive systematizations, namely, the possibility of the scientific study of behavior.

In general, then, we can descry how it is entirely possible to take the behavior of a person as a scientific subject matter, formulate the pre-empirical constraints on that subject matter, and formulate hypothetical or empirical behavioral patterns and regularities in any degree of generality or specificity, complexity, or simplicity (and later we may add, any degree of "depth," meaningfulness, or automatism). We have seen what some of the pre-empirical constraints are. Clearly, the next step is to present an actual pre-empirical formulation of human behavior which meets the conceptual requirements. This will be a major concern in the monograph which follows, tentatively titled *The Behavior of Persons*.

REFERENCES

•

1. Cody, A. B
   "Can a Single Action Have Different Descriptions?"
   Inquiry, Volume 10 (1967), 164–80.

2. Cohen, M. D.
   "The Same Action."
   Proceedings of the Aristotelian Society, Volume 70, (1970),
   75–90.
   London: Methuen & Co., Ltd., 1970.

3. Davidson, D.
   "The Logical Form of Action Sentences"
   in
   Rescher, N. (ed.).
   The Logic of Decision and Action.
   Pittsburgh: University of Pittsburgh Press, 1967.

4. Dray, W.
   Laws and Explanation in History.
   London: Oxford University Press, 1957.

5. Garfinkel, H.
   "Conditions of Successful Degradation Ceremonies"
   in
   Manis, J. G. and Meltzer, B. N. (eds.).

Symbolic Interaction: A Reader in Social Psychology.
Boston: Allyn and Bacon, 1967.

6. Gruner, R.
"The Notion of an Historical Event, I."
Aristotelian Society Supplementary Volume 43 (1969), 141–52.
London: Harrison & Sons, Ltd., 1969.

7. Hall, C. S. and Lindzey, G.
Theories of Personality.
New York: John Wiley & Sons, Inc., 1971.

8. Honderich, T.
"A Conspectus of Determinism, I."
Aristotelian Society Supplementary Volume 43 (1970) 191–216.
London: Aristotelian Society, 1970.

9. Minsky, M.
"Matter, Mind, and Models."
Proceedings of the IFID Congress (1965), Volume 1, 45–49.

10. Ossorio, P.
Persons.
Los Angeles: Linguistic Research Institute, 1966a.

11. Ossorio, P.
Outline of Behavior Description.
Los Angeles: Linguistic Research Institute, 1966b.

12. Ossorio, P.
Notes on Behavior Description.
Los Angeles: Linguistic Research Institute, 1969a.

13. Ossorio, P.
Meaning and Symbolism.
Los Angeles: Linguistic Research Institute, 1969b.

14. Ossorio, P.
    State of Affairs Systems: Theory and Technique for Automatic Fact Analysis (RADC-TR-71-102).
    Rome, N.Y.: Rome Air Development Center, 1971.

15. Ossorio, P.
    "Never Smile at a Crocodile."
    Journal for the Theory of Social Behavior, Volume 3 (1973), 121–40.

16. Skinner, B. F.
    Verbal Behavior.
    New York: Appleton-Century-Crofts, 1957.

17. Walsh, W. H.
    "The Notion of an Historical Event, II."
    Aristotelian Society Supplementary Volume 43 (1969), 153–64.
    London: Harrison and Sons, Ltd., 1969.

INDEX

•

210

Human Model, xi–xiv, 15. *See also* Person concept

Hypothetical objects, processes, etc., 25–26, 69; ultimate particles, etc., *see* Zilch particles

Identification, 84–86, 139, 160, 163, 165, 168, 188–94, 196–203. *See also* Identity coordination; Name; Reidentification

Identity coordination, 20–21, 77, 83. *See also* "The Same Thing"

Identity thesis, 103–12.

Individuals, *see* Basic Object Unit; Basic Process Unit; State-of-Affairs Unit

Inference, 16, 36, 41, 90.

Information, 93–94, 142, 144–45. *See also* Being informative; Formulation

Irrationality, 142, 144.

I–Thou, 152, 154.

James, William, 22.

Kant, Emanuel, 17.

Kenny, Anthony, 83.

Knowledge, 11, 122, 124, 126, 128–29, 140, 165, 169–70, 200. *See also* Self-knowledge

Language, 9, 35, 37, 39, 65, 95, 118, 169, 188; commitment, 37, 56, 95–97, 106, 121; conventions, 5–6, 117, 139; referential, 54, 73, 93, 189, 197–98, 201 (*see also* Reference, theory of); technical, 65, 67, 96–99, 122, 157, 176, 188–89, 196–97; ways of talking, 5, 36–37, 79, 90, 98–99, 159, 174, 181–83, 186, 200–1. *See also*

Behavior, verbal; Statements; Utterance

Lawfulness, 101–2.

Levels of organization, 101–3.

Limit setting, 31, 147.

Limiting cases, 29–31, 33–34, 40–41, 44, 47–48, 105, 132, 180, 202; Limiting Case-I, 29–30, 34, 54, 56, 91–92, 94, 101, 115, 121, 123, 183.

Lindzey, Gardner, 82.

Locus of application, 166–68, 176–77, 192, 201; of study, 167–68, 192–93.

Logic, 174.

Logical relations, 40, 45, 80, 85–86, 96, 107, 138, 147, 151, 185, 196. *See also* Reality concepts, logical relations among

Logical space, 94.

Manipulation, 4, 96, 118–20, 161.

Meaning, 20, 73.

Means-ends description, 58–60, 118–19.

Mechanism, 112, 120, 122–25, 128, 134, 179, 182, 184–85.

Mental process, 16, 103, 105–8. *See also* Identity thesis

Methodological facts, 34–35, 135, 183; issues, 89, 131, 135–36; perspective, 36, 137–38, 141, 143, 185.

Methodology, 13, 34–35, 91, 138–41, 143, 181, 191; scientific, 8, 11–14, 138, 144, 155, 158; and theory, 33–34, 36, 130–31, 137–38, 144, 183. *See also* Connections, real world and science; Statements, methodological status of; Status, methodological; Substantive content and methodological status

Minsky, M., 120, 122, 124–25, 136, 143, 178.

212

213

Social organization, 56; practice, 10, 45, 47, 61, 127, 158, 190.
Sociology of knowledge, 11, 124.
Stage, stage-option, *see* Basic Process Unit
State of Affairs, concept of, 20, 29–31, 53–54, 56–57, 65; concepts, *see* Reality concepts; description, 23–25, 57, 59, 78; unit, 64–70.
State-of-Affairs system, 27, 33, 38, 41, 64, 71–72, 78, 88–89, 112, 158; as calculational, formal, 18–20, 24–26, 28, 64–70, 76, 156. *See also* Calculational system; Conceptual system
Statements, xv, 10, 37, 65, 93–94; methodological status of, 4–6, 9, 130, 137, 139–41, 153, 183.
Status, xvi, 4–6, 17, 117–18, 126, 128–30, 145–51, 158, 174, 181; change of, 47, 131–32, 134–35, 145, 149 (*see also* Accreditation; Degradation ceremony); methodological, 5, 8–9, 28, 33–34, 96, 138–41, 187 (*see also* Methodology; Substantive content and methodological status); second-order, 154.
Status assignment, 5–6, 141, 145–55, 164, 187; self-status-assignment, 148–50, 155. *See also* Degradation ceremony; Self-concept
Stimulus-response, 11, 122, 165, 183–84.
Structural constraints, 46.
Subject matter, 61. *See also* Behavioral science, subject matter; Being informative; History; Identification
Substantive content, 12, 138–39, 142, 168; and methodological status, 6, 33, 137–39, 141, 158–59, 187; re determinism, 89, 126, 128, 131,

135. *See also* Connections, real world and science; Status, methodological
Supernaturalism, 185–87.
Systems, 56. *See also* Calculational system; Conceptual system; Formal system; State-of-Affairs system
Systems theory, 182.

Task analysis, 59–62, 119.
Technology, 119, 123, 165–66, 185.
Teleology, 115.
Temporal succession formula, 114, 117–18.
Theology, 32, 100, 122–23, 126, 130, 158, 178, 186.
Theory, 36, 109, 113, 140–41, 143, 155, 164–67, 182, 197–98; universal, 140, 164. *See also* Methodology and theory; Scientific theory
Third-person approach, 174–76, 178, 180–81, 184.
Totalities, 31–32, 147, 168–69, 172–73.
Transition rules, 18–27, 29, 38–39, 54, 67, 76, 83, 96, 103; specific applications, 35, 40–41, 43, 51, 54–57, 62–66.
Truth, xiii–xv, 5, 36, 71, 82, 97–98, 109, 122, 128, 132–33, 159; eligibility for status of, 5, 65, 71, 97, 114, 129, 134, 136, 154–55.

Ultimates, 31–33, 100, 107. *See also* Objects, ultimate; Zilch particles
Uniqueness, 57 58.
Unity of the Sciences, 80, 100.
Utterance, 189, 194.

Values, 48–50, 60, 132–33, 138, 151, 184. *See also* Truth

215

Version, *see* Basic Process Unit
Volition, 91, 94–95, 124–25.

Walsh, W., 75–77, 79.
Ways of talking, *see* Language, ways of talking
Whorf, Benjamin Lee, 115.
Wick, Warner, 126.
Wisdom, J. O., 125.
Wittgenstein, Ludwig, 69, 94, 125, 135.

World, 31, 33, 73, 147, 155–56, 182, 184, 198; formula, 26, 30, 57, 77, 79, 91, 94, 114, 116, 121; as machine, *see* Mechanism; possible, 7, 26, 35. *See also* Domain; Real world

Zilch particles, 90–94, 99, 101, 112, 122. *See also* Composition and decomposition